Writing with Authors Kids L♥VE!

**Writing Exercises by Authors
of Children's Literature**

Writing

with

**Authors
Kids
L♥VE!**

**Edited by
Kathryn Lee Johnson**

ISBN 1-882664-40-X

Prufrock Press
P.O. Box 8813
Waco, TX 76714-8813
Phone: 800.998.2208 • Fax: 800.240.0333
E-mail: prufrock@prufrock.com
http://www.prufrock.com

For
Jacob and Cliff, the two young writers I love.

Table of Contents

Yes, it's hard to write, but it's harder not to.
—Carl Van Doren

Introduction

Children are filled with imagination and stories. When you encourage them to create and tell their stories, you provide them with meaningful opportunities to learn about themselves, about others, and about their world. Every day in your classrooms you can recognize the important role of early, positive writing experiences. Writing keeps alive children's natural interests, motivation, and enthusiasm for learning. Through writing, your students learn to wonder, think, imagine, explore, and create.

Learning to write is not always easy. Writing is one of the most important, yet complex and challenging, skills that students can master. Teaching children to write is an equally challenging task. To meet this challenge, teachers need instructional resources that are practical and effective. Who could help you teach writing better than writers themselves?

Twenty notable authors of children's literature, including award-winners, provided exercises that focus on various aspects of the writing process. These authors developed excellent ideas and practical suggestions about writing, some of which are based on their books. They offer effective strategies on how to motivate children to become successful writers. Many of these authors are educators who visit with young writers in classrooms all over the country. Both you and your students will benefit from their insight, experience, and knowledge.

Purpose

This compilation of writing exercises is intended to supplement your curriculum. It offers teachers and students creative ideas and innovative lessons that make writing fun. Because writing is a developmental process, you can use the exercises across grade levels and adapt them in a variety of ways to meet the needs of your students. Use the instructional activities to introduce a new idea, practice and strengthen a skill, or enhance the understanding of the literature being studied.

Organization

The lessons are organized into seven easy-to-use chapters: **Finding Ideas** focuses on beginning to write, stimulating students' interests, and finding stories to tell or experiences to describe.

Introduction

The chapter titled **Setting** helps students practice the power of detail and see the relationship between the place of a story and the plot. What happens in a story depends a great deal on the setting.

Writing in the Curriculum Content Areas combines research and writing in other subjects, such as history, science, and geography. Factual picture books as well as nonfiction books can be great resources for collecting and organizing information into various kinds of writing. These could include writing letters or journals from the perspective of historical characters, writing descriptive prose that incorporates factual information, and creating class books.

The chapter on **Plot and Character** examines how these two elements of a story interact effectively. When strong characters are developed, action follows.

The next two chapters explore the language of writing. **Creating Images** looks at the connections between unlike objects and allows readers to see clear pictures in their minds. Metaphors and similes can set a mood and enhance composition. In **Writing Poetry**, authors encourage students to listen, use their senses, notice details, and play with words, sounds, rhythms, and riddles.

In the final chapter, **Editing**, the exercise asks students to think about the question, "How do you know when the story is finished?" This lesson underscores the importance of editing as a natural conclusion to writing.

Students will enjoy getting to know the authors and learning about how they write stories. Lessons include a photograph, a list of publications, and information about each author, such as place of birth, education and favorite activities. Of particular value to students is the advice authors give to young writers. You may share the information about the authors with students as well as encourage students to communicate with them directly using the "Contacting Authors" section in the Appendices.

Research on Writing

Before they enter school, most children already have a clear understanding that written words are important, that writing has meaning and communicates information, requiring particular form and characters (Hall, 1987). Research on writing leads us to conclude that the natural enthusiasm and motivation young children have about beginning to write can be nurtured, encouraged, and developed with the right classroom conditions and climate (Taylor, Blum, & Logston, 1986).

Highlighted below are several important conclusions drawn from what we know about how children learn to write. The research about writing with children in the classroom emphasizes the following points:

- Writing about reading helps students become better readers (Calkins, 1994).

- Increased reading tends to result in better writing (Cox, Shanahan, & Sulzby, 1990).

- To expand children's writing horizons, teachers must involve children in a full range of genres (fiction, biography, fantasy, folk tales, and so forth). Teach the characteristics of each form and assign writing tasks that illustrate those characteristics (Downing, 1995).

- Conferencing is a powerful tool for changing children's perceptions of writing and revision. Create a setting that nurtures (rather than only corrects) the writer (Bury, 1993).

- Teachers can play a significant role in releasing a child's potential for revision. What the teacher emphasizes in revising is what students tend to do (Graves, 1983).

- Teachers can help children see that writing conventions are opportunities for enhancing the meaning of what they want to say (Graves, 1995).

- What young children write about and how they approach writing is more important than their mechanics of writing (spelling, penmanship, punctuation, and spacing; Morrow, 1989).

Introduction

- Classrooms that are literacy oriented nearly always have a physically literate environment (books, magazines, songs, examples of good writing, mailboxes, places to read, places to access writing tools, writing centers, and so forth) (Reutzel & Cooter, 1990).

- Writing is not "deskwork"; it is "lifework" (Calkins, 1994).

Facilitating Writing in the Classroom

Based on research and the knowledge that writing is a developmental process, what can you do to cultivate writing? There are many excellent sources available on effective teaching strategies that facilitate the developmental process of learning to write. Here's are several strategies that, in combination with lessons from this book will build a supportive environment for developing competent young writers.

- Give writing an important emphasis in your class by making it part of the regular, daily routine.

- Make each child feel accepted and valued as a person with important and relevant ideas to express.

- Respect students' struggles, fears, anxieties, and doubts about learning to write. Acknowledge their frustrations and express confidence in their potential.

- Give plenty of time for writing. Good writing is a result of good thinking. Allow time for thoughts and ideas to incubate.

- Vary writing assignments: poetry, essay, letter, advertisement, descriptive paragraph, short story, summary, and so forth.

- Write along with students. Model that you think writing is important enough for you to spend time doing it with them. Share your writing and enthusiasm.

- Give students the freedom to take risks, to explore ideas, and to write honestly without fear of mistakes or criticism.

- Use large group brainstorming sessions to get ideas flowing.

- Allow students to write in collaborative groups to combine ideas.

- Plan time for all writers to read their writings aloud in small or large groups.

- Schedule periodic conferencing times with each student.

- Use the children's literature to model specific elements of writing, such as dialogue, plot, character development, and mechanics.

- Have varied writing sessions: direct them to write quickly, slowly, non-stop for five minutes, in small groups, in large groups, independently, with a teacher, with a parent or older student, at a learning center, at desks, curled up in a corner with a clipboard, at the computer, in a journal, outside, with music, with Gregorian Chants, with a recording of natural sounds, with a flashlight in the dark.

A Final Note

Teaching children to write affords you the special opportunity to appreciate our students as they compose an unusual phrase, a unique expression, an invented word, a funny rhythm. My goal in developing this book was to help educators make writing a positive experience in the classroom. I hope that *Writing with Authors Kids Love!* encourages you to create effective and meaningful writing activities for students. In the art of writing, may each of you experiment, explore, wonder, and learn. But most of all, simply enjoy!

Kathryn Lee Johnson
Editor

Finding Ideas

*The greatest part of a writer's time is spent in reading, in order
to write; a man will turn over half a library to make one book.*

—Samuel Johnson (1709–1784)

*I always write a good first line,
but I have trouble in writing the others.*

—Moliére (1622–1673)

Chapter One

Artie Ann Bates

Photo by Will Herrick

Birthplace: Blackey, KY

Education: University of Kentucky

Enjoys: being with family, gardening, canning vegetables, making jam, cooking and creating new recipes, reading (especially human-interest stories), and writing

Artie Ann grew up in the Appalachian area of eastern Kentucky where she still lives with her husband and child. She plays an important role in her community as a physician, writer, teacher, and activist.

Ragsale is Artie Ann's first book, which is based on her childhood memories. Ragsales were an important part of her childhood and Artie Ann wrote this story to help preserve her Appalachian culture and heritage for children of today.

"Ragsales are a special kind of used clothing store, and when I was a little girl we went to the ragsale every weekend. Wearing used clothes is a way of not wasting things that are still good. Where there used to be a lot of ragsales in eastern Kentucky, there aren't many now, but going to them is as much fun as ever."

She collaborated with another Appalachian artist, Jeff Chapman-Crane, to create an authentic look at a day of ragsalin'.

Advice for Writers:

Read a lot. Keep a journal. Write in any form that is possible for what your schedule allows: letters, poems, recipes, notes. Have other creative outlets to keep your mind in a creative mode.

Artie Ann Bates

Ragsale by Artie Ann Bates (1995)
Illustrated by Jeff Chapman-Crane
Reprinted by permission of Houghton Mifflin Company
ISBN: 0-395-70030-2

Introduction:

How do you get started? A good rule of thumb for writing is to think about what *you* enjoy reading. Different ideas work for different people. Even for the same person, an activity will help sometimes and others times it will not. We have to be open to the subtle things inside that tell us what we might want to write about, say, and read.

Exercise:

Here is a list of possible beginnings I have used that may help stimulate your students' thinking. You may give them one or two of these ideas each day to help them get into a regular routine of writing.

1.   Tell what you dreamed about last night.

   •   Tell it all:
      – colors
      – people
      – smells
      – and even the scary things

2.   Pick an animal and let it talk to another animal that it could be friends with (or, perhaps, could NOT be friends with).

3.   Describe a person that you know well but who is not like you very much (your grandmother, maybe).

   •   Tell why she is different. For example, how was the world different when she grew up?

   •   Did she grow up without some things that you take for granted, such as computers or television?

   •   How did that make her life different in the things she did, how she spent her time, or how she viewed the world?

4.   Think of a place you like to go to and describe it by using all five senses.

Getting Started

Artie Ann Bates

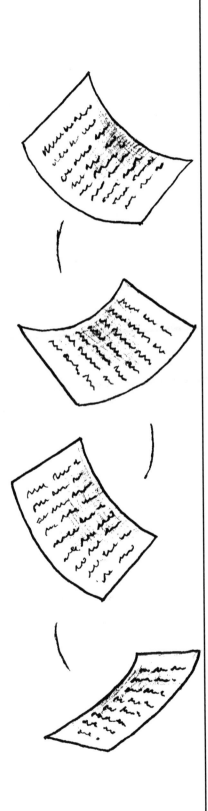

- Tell about:
  - smells, scents, odors;
  - how it looks, describe details of what you see;
  - how you feel when you walk or sit down there;
  - the sounds you hear; and
  - the foods you eat or the drinks you have.

5. To elaborate on number 4 above, go to that place with a pen and notebook and stay for a while. Write about the surroundings using your senses.

6. Listen to two people talking when they do not know that you are listening.

   - For example, listen to your parents discussing the news, going to the doctor, taking care of your grandparents, or talking about events in their day.

   - Write down pieces of their conversation as they talk.

   - Do the same thing in a restaurant sometime.

   - Write down what people say, including their natural expressions, such as "Oh, dear," and "Surely not."

7. Write about something you hate, including the reasons why you hate it.

8. Ask your grandfather (or an elderly individual) what sport he played in high school.

   - Ask him to tell you some of the things that happened to him while playing that sport.

   - Have him compare how the sport was then to how the sport is today.

9. Write three or four paragraphs about your favorite sport in terms of the accidents and injuries that occur while playing it.

10. Write about something you saw that was so scary you cannot talk out loud about it.

11. Write about the different kinds of dirt. (You may have to dig to get some answers!)

   • Students may bring dirt samples in Ziploc® bags from various places.

   • Look, observe, smell, and feel. Describe.

12. Keep a notebook by your bed with a pen and flashlight.

   • After the lights are out and you are relaxed and trying to go to sleep, write down the thoughts that come into your mind, even if they do not make sense.

   • Explain to your parents what you are doing.

13. In your notebook, before you go to bed, jot down the date, the weather for that day, and a few things that happened. This way, you are writing down history.

14. Write about a person who has been dead for a long time. Interview people who knew the person. Find out interesting stories. If possible, go on a research journey:

   • **County Courthouse**—find the birth date and marriage date in the census books, look up when and where the person owned land in the deed books.

   • **Education Department**—find out what schools this person attended.

   • **Newspaper Office**—find out if he or she was ever mentioned in the newspaper. What was written about this person? What did he or she do?

   Then, write a report starting with the person's birth. Take your report all the way through the individual's life telling

Artie Ann Bates

about how many brothers and sisters were in the family, the age when married, life's work, activities in retirement, cause of death, and so forth. When finished, you will have researched and written a *biography*.

15. Read a newspaper editorial and then write an article about it. Tell if you agree or disagree with the writer, and why.

The writing possibilities are endless. This is a beginning and will get students off to a good start!

Book Published:

Bates, A. A. (1995) *Ragsale.* Boston: Houghton Mifflin Company.

Sally Derby

Birthplace: Dayton, OH

Education: Western College for Women

Enjoys: writing, reading, walking, and visiting grandchildren

Advice for Writers:

"For me, the hardest part of writing is finding the story that I want to tell. It takes a lot of patient waiting, writing "first" sentences, waiting for the story to suggest itself. If I'm patient and receptive an idea will come.

Some of the best ideas come from everyday life. You don't have to live in exotic places or have exciting adventures to find something to write about.

Good luck!"

On a snowy Sunday in January, some 50 years ago, I read my first "Maida" book, one of a series about a group of friends who had all sorts of fabulous adventures together. After reading all afternoon, I was so enchanted by the world I had been introduced to that I decided when I grew up I would create my own worlds—I would write books.

I was in the third grade at Edwin D. Smith School in Dayton, OH, on that snowy day, and I have lived in southern Ohio all my life. During high school and college, I prepared myself to write, but my senior year in college I met Karl Miller and decided I'd take time out to get married. In the years following, Karl and I had five sons and then a daughter. The writing was postponed—for years.

Today, now that the children are all grown, I can devote myself full time to writing. It is a joy and a frustration all at once. I truly enjoy writing, but nothing that I write is as good as I thought it would be when I began it. There are so many splendid books for children that I despair of ever being able to equal them. Take

Katherine Paterson, Lois Lowry—think of Natalie Babbitt's *Tuck Everlasting*, or Sylvia Waugh's *The Mennyms*—consider notable picture books like *Millions of Cats* by Wanda Gàg.

Some days when I sit down at my computer and have no ideas in mind at all, I wonder why I keep writing my own stories, why I'm just not content reading books like these. But then I'll think of a name or a sentence or a place, and a story begins to come. And that is so exciting!

Where do the ideas come from? They come from what I see, what I remember, what I hope for. I find that one of the best ways to get ideas is to take long walks. Ironing is good, too. Anything where your body is moving but you don't have to think about what you are doing. I read once of a writer who got her best ideas while she scrubbed the kitchen floor, but I'm not enthusiastic about trying that!

Thinking about the books I have published, I realize that the idea for *The Mouse Who Owned the Sun* came from a conversation about logic that my husband and I had almost 40 years ago. *Jacob and the Stranger* owes its mysterious plant to a picture in a reader when I was in grade school. When my granddaughter, Jessica, got a splinter in her foot while playing hide-and-seek at our house, the incident suggested *King Kenrick's Splinter*. And the game described in *My Steps* is one I played when I was a little girl.

Sally Derby

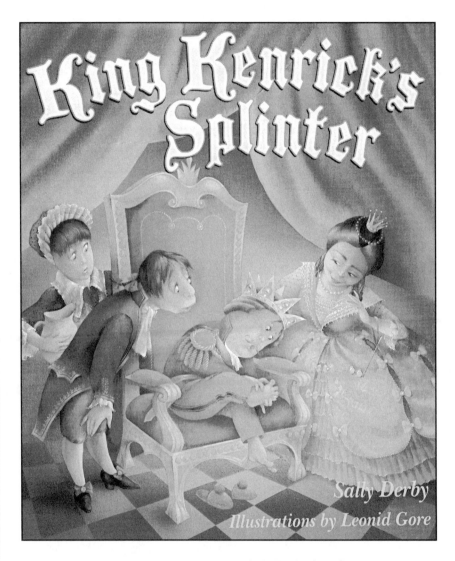

King Kenrick's Splinter by Sally Derby (1994)
Illustrated by Leonid Gore
Reprinted by permission of Walker & Co.
ISBN: 0-8027-8323-6

Introduction:

"The longest journey begins with a single step." The idea of writing a story can be intimidating to students because they are accustomed to reading stories in their finished form. What they don't realize is that sometimes the writer may have begun the story with the same fears and doubts that they are experiencing. "I don't know what to write about." "I don't have any ideas."

This exercise is one way I break through the fear when I can't get started.

Exercise:

1. The teacher should let the students voice their fears freely. Then the teacher might say something like: "Okay, writing a story is difficult. But you can write a sentence—you've been doing that for years. What I want you to do is to write some individual sentences, sentences that might begin stories. You don't need to write what comes next, just a first sentence."

2. Have students write some of these first sentences:

    •   Write a sentence that might begin a fairy story.

    •   Now, write a sentence that would begin a Halloween story.

    •   How about one that could begin a funny story.

    •   Suppose you were going to write about a really mean man. Write the first sentence of this story.

    •   Other first sentence ideas …

3. Take the students through this process for seven or eight sentences. Tell them to save and think about these sentences for a day or two.

Sally Derby

4. In a subsequent lesson, ask the students to pick their favorite first sentence and write two sentences that might follow it. It is likely that doing this will give the students enough of a beginning for their stories that they can develop them.

   (Note the benefit of a day or two of gestation while the students have their sentences put away. Don't omit this part of the process, but don't let it go on too long. Two days maximum is recommended.)

5. If, at this point, the students are still having difficulties, let them choose other first sentences to add to. It is the **process**, not the **product** that is most important.

Sally Derby

Books Published:

Derby, S. (1993). *The Mouse Who Owned the Sun.* New York: Four Winds Press.

Derby, S. (1994). *Jacob and the Stranger.* New York: Ticknor & Fields.

Derby, S. (1994). *King Kenrick's Splinter.* New York: Walker and Company.

Derby, S. (1996). *My Steps.* New York: Lee and Low Books Inc.

Jerrie Oughton

Never give up! You never know if success is right around the corner. I wrote for 35 years before a book was published.

Photo by Charles W. Kenney

Birthplace: Atlanta, GA

Education: Meredith College

Enjoys: reading, movies, sports, and being with children

I was born in Atlanta, GA, but grew up in Arkansas, Tennessee, and North Carolina. When I was 7, I was asked to write a book review and became hooked on seeing my words in print. Then my mother sealed my fate. One day, I overheard her tell my father, "Be careful what you say around Jerrie Lynn. She might grow up to be a writer and tell it all." I did. I do. A high school teacher, Mrs. Peacock, made me even more interested in becoming a writer because she read such powerful stories and poems to our class. I dedicated my first book to her. She is my hero, now in her 90s. Not everyone has a Mrs. Peacock. I'm glad I did.

Today, I write on my lunch hours, after work, and sometimes from nine until midnight. I no longer teach, but I am a secretary so that when I complete my seven hour day at work, I don't bring any work home. I laughingly say, "I would do almost anything. I would deliver pizza if it would allow me time to write."

My husband and I have five children and three grandchildren. Often, I write about people in my family or those I know or have known. I don't use real instances, but the people are real.

Jerrie Oughton

Every part of writing is my favorite at the time I am doing it. To begin a novel, I get a large brown envelope to stuff full of random ideas and bits of conversation I like or names of people that interest me. When it gets so full it is almost bursting, and when I feel so full of this story I could burst, then I must sit down and write. First, a draft by hand. Then polish. Then off to my editor. More polishing and changing. If I am fortunate, the last thing I have to do is proofread the galleys ... which means my editor bought the story.

When I am not writing on paper, I am writing in my head. Of course, I enjoy visiting schools and talking with students about their dreams. I enjoy reading, going to movies, watching sports and, most of all, being with children ... mine and other people's.

Jerrie Oughton

How the Stars Fell into the Sky by Jerrie Oughton (1992)
Illustrated by Lisa Desimini
Reprinted by permission of Houghton Mifflin Company
ISBN: 0-395-58798-0

National
Council of
Social Studies
Award

California
Children's
Media Award

Smithsonian's
Celebration of
the Best

Focus:

Dialogue, characterization, opening sentence, and setting.

Introduction:

The purpose of this lesson is two-fold. First, it jump-starts a student into writing. Second, it gives students the confidence to launch out and write, even when they don't quite know where the writing is going.

When writing fiction, it is invaluable to have enough confidence to face a blank page with only the melody of the song playing through one's mind. Having confidence that the words will come in their own good time is the hope-giver of all writers.

Sometimes a sack lunch can hold wonderful treats. Things to eat so satisfying that you sit back and think of that lunch later. Today we are going to pack a sack *launch*. It can be just as satisfying in its own way as that sack lunch. Here's how.

Exercise:

I am placing a brown paper bag on your desk—a sack. Your assignment is this: When I complete your instructions, follow me to the playground.

1. Pick up things of interest to you and put them in your sack. *Don't show anyone* what is in your sack. Keep it a secret.

    •   A bottle cap may not turn Mary on in the least, but Jim might remember the very first Coca-Cola® he ever drank. It was at a Reds' game with his grandfather when he was 7. He even recalled something his grandfather said to him.

2. After about 10 minutes on the playground, come in and store your sack in your desk.

Jerrie Oughton

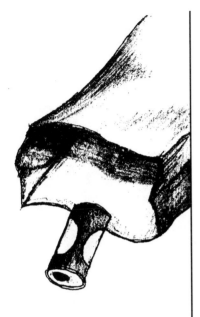

3. On your way home from school or in your house and yard, collect more.

4. You can scribble down conversations you hear or things you see on your way home from school. If you hear something really interesting, something that makes you sit up and listen, write it down. It might be a strong opening line.

After a few days of collecting and writing, direct students to:

5. Get a piece of paper and your sack. Reach in the sack and pull out one item.

6. Begin writing the first thing that comes into your mind. When you run out of words, pull out another item. You may surprise yourself at how much can come from one small thing.

7. Read what you have written. Do you want to change it? Feel free. Work with it like a piece of modeling clay until you have made something you feel good about.

Examples:

A fifth-grade girl found a feather on the playground which reminded her of her grandmother who kept canaries. Her entire piece was about her grandmother. She brought her sack to class to share with anybody who might be stuck and needed more items.

A sixth-grade boy, upon finding an aluminum can, told of a summer vacation with his family. They got 35 miles down the road and had to turn around and go back home because the car broke down. After paying the towing fee, all his mother had left in her purse was enough to buy drinks for everybody. A penny he picked up reminded him of the tight times his family had while his father completed medical school.

Books Published:

Oughton, J (1992) *How the Stars Fell into the Sky*. New York: Houghton Mifflin Company.

Oughton, J. (1994). *The Magic Weaver of Rugs*. New York: Houghton Mifflin Company.

Oughton, J. (1995). *Music from a Place Called Half Moon*. New York: Houghton Mifflin Company.

Oughton, J. (1997). *The War in Georgia*. New York: Houghton Mifflin Company.

Ann Whitford Paul

" If you are think-ing about being a writer, read as much as you can. Also take classes from other writers. Be willing to revise your writing over and over again to make it better.

My best advice is to write about what you know. Ideas are all around you. Trust that if a sub-ject interests you, it will interest others. "

Photo by Donna Zweig

Birthplace: Evanston, IL

Education: University of Wisconsin
               Columbia University, M.S.W.

Enjoys: quilting, knitting, walking, reading, and cooking

Born in Evanston, IL, I was the oldest child in a family of five children. I am not one of those writers who always knew she want-ed to write, but I did always read ... hiding under the piano, sitting on a window seat, or with a flashlight late at night in bed.

Other than school assignments and thank you letters for Christmas and birthday gifts, the only writing I ever did was to sporadically keep a diary ... until a friend stole it and read all my secrets!

My father's work moved him around a lot, so I attended sever-al different elementary and secondary schools outside Chicago, IL, Philadelphia, PA, and Madison, WI. I attended Northwestern University and graduated from the University of Wisconsin with a B. A. in sociology and Columbia University with a master's degree in social work. For four years, I worked in New York City at an adoption agency and in a hospital where I met my husband, Ron, a thoracic surgeon.

Ann Whitford Paul

It was my four children who gave me the inspiration to write. When they were young, ours was a hectic and noisy home. I looked forward to that time each day before nap or bedtime when we would sit together in a rocking chair, or snuggle close on a bed and read. I loved those quiet times so much I thought there must be nothing more wonderful to do than write books that other parents and children could share. Fortunately, I live near a large university where I was able to take classes from such wonderful writers as Sue Alexander, Sonia Levitin, and Myra Cohn Livingston.

Today, just one of my children still lives at home so I have plenty of time to write while she is in school and at after-school activities. My two books, *Eight Hands Round: A Patchwork Alphabet* and *The Seasons Sewn: A Year in Patchwork* grew out of a life-long interest in the way people used to live and my hobby of sewing patchwork. The idea for *Shadows Are About* came on one of my daily walks.

Because it is important to me to write every day, I even snatch times on the weekend to work. Wherever I go, I carry a small pad of paper and a pen in case an idea comes to me.

Ann Whitford Paul

THE SEASONS SEWN

Written by Ann Whitford Paul

Illustrated by Michael McCurdy

A YEAR IN PATCHWORK

The Seasons Sewn by Ann Whitford Paul (1996)
Illustrated by Michael McCurdy
Reprinted by permission of Harcourt Brace & Company
ISBN: 0-15-276918-8

1996
Carl Sandburg
Award for
Children's
Literature

New York
Times Best
Illustrated
Books of the
Year

Introduction:

"Help! I have nothing to write about!"

Not so. You have many things to write about. You just don't know how to find them. The purpose of this lesson is to stimulate your creative thinking to find not only a subject but a focus for your writing.

Many students feel confused and afraid when given a writing assignment. This exercise will help you find the direction your writing should take, whether your teacher assigns a specific subject or leaves the subject up to you.

Exercise:

1. At the top of the page, write the subject of your assignment, or the subject of your choice. (See example on next page.)

2. Draw a vertical line down the center of the page. At the top of the left side of the page write the word "facts." On the top of the right side of the page write the word "feelings."

3. Under "facts" quickly jot down what you know about the subject using all of your senses (sight, touch, taste, smell, and sound).

4. Under "feelings" write any thoughts or memories that the subject brings to mind.

5. You will be surprised at the images that will come to you. As you write these facts and feelings you will notice that one is more appealing to you, either because it brings up strong positive or strong negative emotions in you. That is what you should write about.

Finding Your Subject

Ann Whitford Paul

Example:

POPCORN

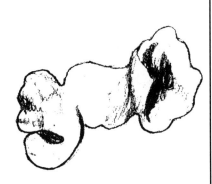

Facts	Feelings
cream color	looks like a small cloud
bumpy	old Sunday family dinners of popcorn and apples
puffy	
	first kiss—after Saturday matinee with popcorn at the movie
jumps up when heated when seed is exposed to heat, it pops and expands	
	chains of popcorn and cranberries at Christmas
small bit of tan from seed	
bland taste	tastes like cardboard
no smell when cold	cows getting loose in the cornfield
"pop-pop" sound when popping	eating corn on the cob with butter dripping down my chin and onto my fingers —greasy napkin
crunchy noise when eating	
need to chew	

Ann Whitford Paul

Books Published:

Paul, A. W. (1985) *Owl at Night*. New York: Putnam.
Paul, A. W. (1991). *Eight Hands Round: A Patchwork Alphabet*. New
   York: HarperCollins.
Paul, A. W. (1992). *Shadows Are About*. New York: Scholastic.
Paul, A. W. (1996). *The Seasons Sewn: A Year in Patchwork*.
   Orlando, FL: Browndeer Press, Harcourt Brace & Company.

Forthcoming Books:

In My Yard
All by Herself
Silly Sadie, Silly Samuel
Hello Toes! Hello Feet!
Everything to Spend the Night

   Ann Whitford Paul's poems have appeared in *Poems for
Grandmothers* and *Dog Poems*, both anthologies edited by Myra
Cohn Livingston, *Snuffles and Snouts* edited by Laura Robb, and
in *Cricket* and *Spider* magazines. Her stories have also appeared in
Highlights and *The Friend*.

Setting

My place is full of words, of settings real and pretend, of people I have never met but know as well as I know myself, of events that never happened but have changed me in their imagining. This is why I write.

—Karen Cushman
from Newbery Metal
Acceptance Speech

Chapter Two

33

Paul Owen Lewis

Photo by Marcia Iverson

Birthplace: La Jolla, CA

Education: Cornish Institute in Seattle
University of Washington

Enjoys: being the first to discover something wonderful, whether through drawing, writing, building, or dreaming

When Paul Owen Lewis was a young boy, his father gave him a toy sailboat, promising his son that later they would buy a real sailboat that the two could sail together. But Paul's father became ill and was never able to buy that promised sailboat. Paul was very disappointed. Then he realized that he could at least draw sailboats. By the time he reached fifth grade, he drew the best sailboats in his class.

Paul earned a degree in fine arts from the Cornish Institute in Seattle and a teaching certificate from the University of Washington. He taught for two years but soon realized that this was not what he wanted to do. He wanted to be an author and illustrator. As an adult he bought an old sailboat, which he refurbished and named *Apogee*.

Paul Owen Lewis

One day while substitute teaching, he met a children's author at the school. Later, he took his portfolio of illustrations to the author's home and asked how he could become an author. He was told "not to make things up that you think will please others. Write for yourself." From this inspiring visit grew Paul's first book, *Davy's Dream*. Just by chance he visited the whale museum at Friday Harbor. He combined his dream of owning his own sailboat with the desire to be among the whales.

Because Paul had been trained as a teacher, he thought that others might be interested to see how an author makes a book. When he visits schools, he shows slides of each step he took in creating his first book. He shares with students exactly how he drew the pictures that became *Davy's Dream*.

Paul is very visual. He sees the story rather than writes the story. As his stories develop, first he draws the illustrations and puts them in the order he wants them, and then he writes the words to go with the pictures. Drawing is his way of writing.

Storm Boy by Paul Owen Lewis (1995)
Reprinted by permission of Beyond Words Publishing Inc.
ISBN: 1-885223-12-9

1996
American
Book Award

Pacific
Northwest
Booksellers
Association
Award

Washington
State
Governor's
Award

Paul Owen Lewis

Ever Wondered?

Discovery consists of looking at the same thing as everyone else and thinking something different.
—Albert Szent Gyorgyi

Purpose:

To generate original topics for writing and have fun with the process.

Introduction:

I don't know about you, but for me the most exciting and rewarding part about being a writer is creating something that no one has ever created before.

You see, when I was a kid, I dreamed about being an astronaut exploring the universe. Now, as a creative writer, I'm living my dream by exploring the uncharted universe of the imagination.

Exercise:

So, how do you do it? How do you create something that no one has ever created before? It's easier than you think. But first, here's a surprise. According to Nobel Prize winning scientist, Albert Szent Gyorgyi, "Discovery consists of looking at the same thing as everyone else and thinking something different."

Yep, that's right, nobody really creates "something from nothing," as I once thought. Instead you "discover" an idea when you take something that already exists, even something familiar, and make it "new" by looking at it in an unfamiliar way.

Step 1

- Ask a "What if?" question.

    - For example, everyone knows something about the ancient Egyptians. Nothing new there, right? But what if you take the Egyptians, along with their distinctive art and architectural style, out of their native desert and place them somewhere completely different, say, the *Arctic*? What could happen?

Step 2

- Choose a familiar subject to write about. Then make a list of everything you can think of that is associated with the subject you have chosen.

    - For example, an Egyptian list might include:

pyramids	Sphinx	mummies
pharaohs	desert	sarcophagus
camels	sand	Nile

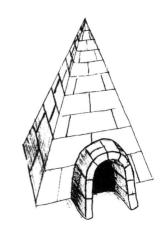

Step 3

- Now, ask yourself the question, "In what ways would a different setting (e.g. the Arctic environment) affect or change these Egyptian things?" Answers can range from the humorous, whimsical, and creative to higher-level thinking and problem-solving. Possible answers might include:

    - Pyramids of ice could be called "pyrigloos."
    - The Sphinx might have the body of a walrus instead of a lion.
    - A mummy may be encased in an ice box instead of a sarcophagus.
    - Would they ride polar bears instead of camels?

- That's just the tip of the ideaberg (pun intended!). The list is endless.

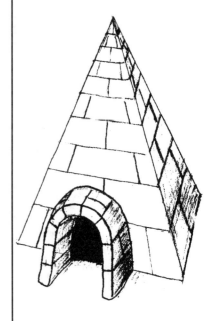

Step 4

- Consider all your discoveries and build some of these details into a narrative following a conventional story pattern.

    - beginning
    - middle
    - end

Paul Owen Lewis

  - character(s)
  - setting
  - conflict and resolution

- Now, you'll be surprised at how creative and original you can be once you have a long list of material to work with!

Ever Wondered? For Explorers, Inventors, and Artists of All Ages
by Paul Owen Lewis

Books Published:

Lewis, P. O. (1988). *Davy's Dream*. Hillsboro, OR: Beyond Words Publishing Inc.

Lewis, P. O. (1989). *The Starlight Bride*. Hillsboro, OR: Beyond Words Publishing Inc.

Lewis, P. O. (1990). *P. Bear's New Year's Party*. Hillsboro, OR: Beyond Words Publishing Inc.

Lewis, P. O. (1993). *Grasper*. Hillsboro, OR: Beyond Words Publishing Inc.

Lewis, P. O. (1995). *Storm Boy*. Hillsboro, OR: Beyond Words Publishing Inc.

Lewis, P. O. (1997). *Frog Girl*. Hillsboro, OR: Beyond Words Publishing Inc.

Materials Published for Educators:

Lewis, P. O. (1991). *Ever Wondered? For Explorers, Inventors, and Artists of All Ages*. Hillsboro, OR: Beyond Words Publishing Inc.

Jill Wheeler

Photo by John Colwell

Birthplace: Sibley, IA

Education: South Dakota State University.

Enjoys: reading, motorcycle riding, playing with my daughter, cooking, traveling, and working out

I grew up on a farm near the small town of Sibley, IA. Farm life is wonderful for kids, but it can be lonely, too. I soon discovered that my imagination, along with my books, was the best way to entertain myself.

My mother introduced me to the wonderful world of reading with the *Little House* series by Laura Ingalls Wilder. I devoured every Laura Ingalls Wilder book I could find. In fact, I read her *Little House* books seven times each. I quickly moved on to discover other authors like Mary Stewart and later, the classics. In fact, as a pre-teen I pined to live in the swashbuckling days of Alexandre Dumas.

When I wasn't reading or helping my family on the farm, I was making up stories in my head. I had my mother's old dollhouse, and I used it as the setting for many a tale. I began writing stories of my own in second grade, and I never got writing out of my system. I wrote for the junior high, then the high school newspapers, and studied journalism at South Dakota State University.

Today, I do a little writing for my job with a marketing communications agency, but mostly I write at night, on weekends, and over my lunch hour. Much of my writing is in the form of letters or journal entries. It's tough to squeeze in time for much else as I also have a young daughter, Anna. I do keep a journal for her to remind myself of the funny things she says and does.

Jill Wheeler

Dr. Seuss by Jill Wheeler (1992)
Reprinted by permission of Abdo & Daughters
ISBN: 1-56239-112-7

Purpose:

To develop story material and establish the importance of place.

Introduction:

Maybe you've heard your students say they want to write but they don't know what to write about. Or perhaps they have a good feel for their characters and plot but they're missing the importance of background and detail in their settings.

This exercise is designed to help students generate material to write about, help them overcome the fear of a blank page, and get them thinking about what an important role place and setting play in writing narratives.

Exercise:

1.   Supply each student with several pages of blank paper and a pen or pencil.

2.   Have students close their eyes and silently answer the following questions:

*   Think about a time in your life when you had a lot of fun.
*   Think about who was with you.
*   Think about what you were doing.
*   Where were you?
*   What did you hear?
*   What did you smell?
*   What did you taste?
*   What time of year was it?
*   Was it hot or cold? Dry or humid?
*   What objects did you touch?
*   What emotions were you feeling?

You may want to offer suggestions; in other words, for "What did you hear?" you might ask students if they heard running water, shouts and screams, or mosquitoes buzzing at the window.

It Was Hot That Day

Jill Wheeler

3. Next, have them write down the answers to the questions you asked. Have them begin by writing "I remember having a lot of fun one time when …" Ask them to describe, in detail, exactly what they were doing, with whom, and where.

4. Tell them they must write constantly for five minutes straight. Even if they have to write "I don't remember anything else" over and over, tell them just to keep their hand moving and keep on writing. Urge them to write down as much as they possibly can remember.

5. When five minutes is over, ask for volunteers to read what they have written.

6. Once a volunteer has read his or her memory, ask the class how the scene could be made into a story. Gather ideas about different stories from the students. They do not have to be true.

    Example:

    A student tells of a day playing with cousins at the family's summer lake cabin. Another student suggests that the children find a mysterious chest at the bottom of the lake. They drag it out of the water but can't get it open. The story involves how they get it open, and what they find.

7. Take one of the story ideas and put it in an opposite setting.

    Example:

    Using the example above, now the student is playing with cousins on a cold, wintry day in the middle of the city. They can't find a chest in the lake now. What story would work instead?

8. Discuss:

- How can a writer make stories out of everyday experiences?
- What do sensory details add to a story?
- How do stories change when the settings change?
- How can writers use place to make a story more interesting?

Jill Wheeler

Books Published:

Wheeler, J. (1988). *Lost in London*. New York: Abdo & Daughters.

Wheeler, J. (1989). *Bound for Boston*. New York: Abdo & Daughters.

Wheeler, J. (1989). *The Story of Crazy Horse*. New York: Abdo & Daughters.

Wheeler, J. (1989). *The Story of Geronimo*. New York: Abdo & Daughters.

Wheeler, J. (1989). *The Story of Hiawatha*. New York: Abdo & Daughters.

Wheeler, J. (1989). *The Story of Pontiac*. New York: Abdo & Daughters.

Wheeler, J. (1989). *The Story of Sequoyah*. New York: Abdo & Daughters.

Wheeler, J. (1989). *The Story of Sitting Bull*. New York: Abdo & Daughters.

Wheeler, J. (1991). *Corazon Aquino*. New York: Abdo & Daughters.

Wheeler, J. (1991). *Earth Day Every Day*. New York: Abdo & Daughters.

Wheeler, J. (1991). *Earth Moves: Get There with Energy to Spare*. New York: Abdo & Daughters.

Wheeler, J. (1991). *The Food We Eat*. New York: Abdo & Daughters.

Wheeler, J. (1991). *Healthy Earth, Healthy Bodies*. New York: Abdo & Daughters.

Wheeler, J. (1991). *Nancy R. Reagan*. New York: Abdo & Daughters.

Wheeler, J. (1991). *The People We Live With*. New York: Abdo & Daughters.

Wheeler, J. (1991). *The Throw-Away Generation*. New York: Abdo & Daughters.

Wheeler, J. (1992). *A. A. Milne: Creator of Winnie the Pooh*. New York: Abdo & Daughters.

Wheeler, J. (1992). *Coretta Scott King*. New York: Abdo & Daughters.

Wheeler, J. (1992). *Dr. Seuss*. New York: Abdo & Daughters.

Wheeler, J. (1992). *Laura Ingalls Wilder*. New York: Abdo & Daughters.

Wheeler, J. (1992). *Michael Landon*. New York: Abdo & Daughters.

Wheeler, J. (1992). *Mother Teresa.* New York: Abdo & Daughters.

Wheeler, J. (1992). *Princess Caroline.* New York: Abdo & Daughters.

Wheeler, J. (1992). *Raisa Gorbachev.* New York: Abdo & Daughters.

Wheeler, J. (1993). *Beastly Neighbors.* New York: Abdo & Daughters.

Wheeler, J. (1993). *Branch Out: A Book about Land.* New York: Abdo & Daughters.

Wheeler, J. (1993). *Earth Kids.* New York: Abdo & Daughters.

Wheeler, J. (1993). *Every Drop Counts: A Book about Water.* New York: Abdo & Daughters.

Wheeler, J. (1993). *For the Birds: A Book about Air.* New York: Abdo & Daughters.

Wheeler, J. (1994). *The Midwest and the Heartland.* New York: Abdo & Daughters.

Wheeler, J. (1994). *The Northeast.* New York: Abdo & Daughters.

Wheeler, J. (1994). *The Pacific West.* New York: Abdo & Daughters.

Wheeler, J. (1994). *The Southeast and Gulf States.* New York: Abdo & Daughters.

Wheeler, J. (1994). *The West.* New York: Abdo & Daughters.

Wheeler, J. (1995). *Louisa May Alcott.* New York: Abdo & Daughters.

Wheeler, J. (1995). *Mark Twain.* New York: Abdo & Daughters.

Wheeler, J. (1996). *Bill Peet.* New York: Abdo & Daughters.

Wheeler, J. (1996). *Judy Blume.* New York: Abdo & Daughters.

Wheeler, J. (1996). *Selena.* New York: Abdo & Daughters.

Wheeler, J. (1996). *Tiger Woods.* New York: Abdo & Daughters.

Wheeler, J. (1996). *Heather Whitestone.* New York: Abdo & Daughters.

Wheeler, J. (1996). *R. L. Stine.* New York: Abdo & Daughters.

Wheeler, J. (1997). *Lloyd Alexander.* New York: Abdo & Daughters.

Wheeler, J. (1997). *Judith Viorst.* New York: Abdo & Daughters.

Wheeler, J. (1997). *Virginia Hamilton.* New York: Abdo & Daughters.

Wheeler, J. (1997). *Gwendolyn Brooks.* New York: Abdo & Daughters.

Wheeler, J. (1997). *L. Frank Baum.* New York: Abdo & Daughters.

Wheeler, J. (1997). *Peggy Parish.* New York: Abdo & Daughters.

Writing in Curriculum Content Areas

We write to taste life twice.

—Anaïs Nin

Chapter Three

Lynne Cherry

Photo by Mi Kim

Birthplace: Philadelphia, PA

Education: Tyler School of Art
Temple University
Yale University, M.A.

Enjoys: traveling, canoeing, exploring little rivers and meanders, forests, my dogs, Rocky and Jasper

Lynne Cherry is an award-winning writer and illustrator with a focus on nature and environmental books. She is the director of the Center for Children's Environmental Literature, a nonprofit organization that strives to make children and teachers aware of the natural world through education and literature. She knows that one person can make a difference in this world and she encourages children to write letters and speak out when they feel strongly about an issue.

Lynne has had artist in residences at the Princeton Center for Energy and Environmental Studies, World Wildlife Fund, the Smithsonian Environmental Research Center in Edgewater, MD, Patuxent Wildlife Research Center, the Marine Biological Institute and Woods Hole Oceanography Institute both in Woods Hole, MA.

Lynne travels to many countries getting ideas for her book illustrations. She enjoys expressing the beauty she sees in life through her art.

Advice for Writers:

"Write about what matters to you. Notice the small details in life—idiosyncrasies of your friends, family, and pets—things that you love about them. Go to your favorite natural place and sit patiently—watch, listen, smell—fine-tune your senses. If you sit long enough something unusual and wonderful will almost always happen. Sit and watch adventures unfold."

Lynne Cherry

Flute's Journey: The Life of a Wood Thrush by Lynne Cherry (1997)
Reprinted by permission of Harcourt Brace & Company.
ISBN: 0-15-292853-7

American Bookseller's Association Pick of the List

Purposes:

To follow the route of a local migratory bird.

To write a descriptive paragraph about a specific migratory bird.

Materials:

Large map of North, Central, and South America
Flute's Journey: The Life of a Wood Thrush by Lynne Cherry
Library resources on migratory birds
Back issues of *National Geographic*
Peterson's Bird Guide

Introduction:

We are a part of a big world filled with different people, traditions, languages, creatures, and climate. By getting to know a local bird and following its migratory route, geography will come alive. This exercise is based on the book *Flute's Journey: The Life of a Wood Thrush*, however, students should choose a local bird to study. (The wood thrush is indigenous—native to much of the central and eastern US.)

Exercise 1: Library Research

1. Read the book *Flute's Journey* aloud. On a map or globe, Have students point out the migration route that Flute followed.

2. Research the migratory birds that live in your area. Have students choose a particular bird to study in-depth.

3. Display a large map of North, Central, and South America on a bulletin board. Have students mark the route of their bird on a large map (use markers or pins and string).

Charting a Migratory Bird Route:
Flute's Journey

Lynne Cherry

Resources:

- *National Geographic* has back issues on migratory birds with large maps showing their routes.

- *Peterson's Bird Guide*

- Call or visit a local nature center to learn about the characteristics of the local birds.

- Have an ornithologist visit the class to discuss local migratory birds.

- Write letters requesting information from the Center for Children's Environmental Literature.

- Contact the Audubon Society for information.

- The best resource is your own back yard. If you do not have a cat, put a feeder in your yard to attract local birds. Identify them in *Peterson's Bird Guide*.

Exercise 2: Writing a Descriptive Paragraph

1. Explain that writers use words to give the reader visual images. Many books have illustrations that allow us to see the story. However, when there are no pictures, we can still "see" with our minds exactly what the writers are describing by the words that they use.

2. Discuss how parts of the story make the reader feel. Did they feel sad when he became ill?

3. Talk about the value of eliciting emotional responses to a story.

4. Review descriptions in *Flute's Journey* that give us clear information about the wood thrush.

Examples:

- Flute had "a few unusual white feathers on his head."
- He nested in a dogwood tree.
- His enemies were cats, raccoons, hawks, black snakes, foxes, and people.
- His song sounded like a flute.
- He ate spicebush and dogwood berries, insects, snails, and slugs.

5. After students have selected and studied local migratory birds, post pictures and information about these birds around the room.

6. Have the students write a descriptive paragraph about their particular bird of interest.

7. Guide their descriptive writing by discussing the elements that might distinguish one bird from another. On the board, list the categories that children mention, such as:

    - physical descriptions (color, size, markings, and so forth);
    - types of trees where they nest;
    - where they migrate and habits;
    - enemies;
    - food; and
    - sounds.

8. After the paragraphs are complete, allow students to read their descriptions aloud.

Variations:

- Have students guess each other's bird based on the descriptions.
- Compare and contrast physical descriptions of birds.
- Make tape recordings of the bird sounds.
- Make collages of the foods that the birds eat.
- Categorize or group the birds in various ways.

Lynne Cherry

For further reading:

One Bird, Two Habitats, by Susan Gilchrist. Wisconsin Department of Natural Resources. Available through training workshops. Contact:
Darrel Covell
University of Wisconsin
1630 Linden Dr., Rm 226
Madison WI 53706
Phone: 608.265.8264 • Fax: 608.262.6099

"Nature's Course" Newsletter, January/February 1997 issue. To order the "Nature's Course" newsletter, send $3.50 to:
Center for Children's Environmental Literature
P. O. Box 5995
Washington, DC 20016

Partners in Flight/Aves de las Americas
NFWF
1120 Connecticut Ave. NW
Suite 900
Washington, DC 20036

Journey North
Share wildlife observations via the Internet, get daily news reports, challenge questions, and online lesson plans.
E-mail: jn-register-info@lerner.org
On the web: http://www.learner.org

Books Written and Illustrated:

Cherry, L. (1988). *Who's Sick Today?* New York: Dutton.

Cherry, L. (1990). *Archie, Follow Me.* New York. Dutton.

Cherry, L. (1990). *The Great Kapok Tree.* San Diego, CA: Harcourt Brace Jovanovich.

Cherry, L. (1992). *A River Ran Wild.* San Diego, CA: Harcourt Brace Jovanovich.

Cherry, L. (1994). *The Armadillo from Amarillo.* San Diego, CA: Harcourt Brace & Company

Cherry, L. (1995). *The Dragon and the Unicorn.* San Diego, CA: Harcourt Brace & Company

Cherry, L. (1997). *Flute's Journey: The Life of a Wood Thrush.* San Diego, CA: Harcourt Brace & Company

Cherry, L. (1998). *Grizzly Bear.* New York: Dutton.

Cherry, L. (1998). *Orangutan.* New York: Dutton.

Cherry, L. (1998). *Seal.* New York: Dutton.

Cherry, L. (1998). *Snow Leopard.* New York: Dutton.

Cherry, L., & Plotkin, M. (1998). *The Shaman's Apprentice.* Harcourt Brace & Company

Illustrated:

Carey, V. (1985). *Harriet and William and the Terrible Creature.* New York: Dutton.

Howard, J. R. (1997). *When I'm Sleepy.* New York: Dutton.

McCormack, J. (1983). *Rabbit Travels.* New York: Dutton.

Meyer, C. (1976). *Coconut: The Tree of Life.* New York: Morrow.

National Wildlife Federation. (1980). *Ranger Rick's Holiday Book.* Washington, DC: Author.

Roberts, J. (1979). *Emir's Education in the Proper Use of Magical Powers.* New York: Delacorte Press.

Roy, R. (1986). *Big and Small, Short and Tall.* New York: Clarion.

Roy, R. (1982). *What Has Ten Legs and Eats Corn Flakes?* New York: Clarion.

Russell, S. P. (1977). *What's the Time, Starling?* New York: McKay.

Ryder, J. (1982). *The Snail's Spell.* New York: F. Warne.

Ryder, J. (1987). *Where Butterflies Grow.* New York: Lodestar.

Van Woerkom, D. (1979). *Hidden Messages.* New York: Crown.

Viorst, J. (1981). *If I Were in Charge of the World and Other Worries.* New York: Atheneum.

Nancy Smiler Levinson

Photo by Irwin A. Levinson

Advice for Writers:

"When you have finished writing your first draft, read your work aloud and listen to what you have written. This will help you hear the "sound" of your language and help you as you begin your rewriting."

Birthplace: Minneapolis, MN

Education: University of Minnesota

Enjoys: reading, going to symphonies, theater, and movies

I was born in Minneapolis, MN, and went to school there, including graduating from the University of Minnesota.

Beginning in my childhood and continuing throughout my life, reading has always provided me with a great source of pleasure. I began to write stories when I was in the fifth grade. In the sixth grade, I wrote my first "novel." I had come under the spell of Nancy Drew. My book, which I wrote on notebook paper, was about a 16-year-old girl (how I aspired to become a glamorous teenager!) who solves a murder aboard an ocean liner on which she was a stowaway.

That was my first and last mystery. Afterward, I concentrated on writing stories that were closer to my heart—the emotional kind that would make a young girl weep.

I have worked as a newspaper reporter, an editor, and a Head Start teacher, but writing books for young readers is the most joyful and challenging work I have ever done. I write fiction and non-fiction. Sometimes I am asked which I like best, and my answer is always "both." I think that writing deals with emotions and feelings. Fiction, such as my book *Clara and the Bookwagon*, allows me such exploration. I enjoy researching and writing nonfiction, particularly history and biographies. I like to write nonfiction so that it reads like a story. My book about the history of women railroaders, *She's Been Working on the Railroad*, is a good example of that.

I write full-time. I also speak to children in classrooms, encouraging them to write, as well as to experience the joys of reading. I have two grown sons. When I am not working, I read, of course, and I like going to the theater, movies, and symphonies.

Nancy Smiler Levinson

Thomas Alva Edison: Great Inventor by Nancy Smiler Levinson (1996)
Reprinted by permission of Scholastic Inc.
ISBN: 0-590-52767-3

Purpose:

To explore first person viewpoint by writing a letter from another individual's perspective.

Skills Practiced:

Research before writing;
Using imagination;
Substantive letter writing; and
Writing from a historical perspective

Introduction:

Discuss in class historical figures and events that have brought about change. Have students read biographies. Review: Writing in the first person means writing from the "I" point-of-view.

Exercise:

1. Students read biographies or about people in a past period.

2. Students write letters as if they were those historical figures. Remind students to imagine themselves as the people who are writing.

3. The aim of the letter is for the figure/writer to convince someone or some group of the future importance of the person's work. Emphasize the need for using details and being specific.

4. Showing students examples of letters-to-the-editor from a newspaper can be helpful.

Sincerely Yours, Thomas Alva Edison:
Writing a Letter

Nancy Smiler Levinson

Example:

Thomas Edison writes a letter to a friend or inventor, explaining what his intended light bulb will mean for the future. This example is based on my book, *Thomas Alva Edison, Great Inventor*. Edison writes to friend, Milt Adams:

Dear friend, Milt,

It was good to receive your last letter. I'm glad to know that you and your family are well.

Yes, it's true what you hear about my latest idea. I intend to invent a glow bulb. It will be an electric bulb. I hope to create a system of electricity that will bring light to people everywhere.

Yes, it's also true that I am being called "crazy," and "an American showoff!" Being called crazy is nothing new. I have never paid attention to what others say about me and my inventions. The important thing is that I continue my work. If something fails, I will try until I achieve it, or at least learn why it won't work.

Believe me, this electric glow bulb will work! And the system of electric lights someday will change the world forever. This new method of lighting will be practical and safe. It will also mean light that is long-lasting. Not like candles or gas lights.

My assistants and I are already at work. I have done thousands of sketches. We'll use a filament and an airless glass to encase the filament. An electric current will pass through a wire and heat the filament. Then we'll have an electric glow!

Well, my friend, there you have it.

Sincerely,

Tom

Other Suggestions:

- **Christopher Columbus** writes to Ferdinand and Isabella, begging sponsorship on a voyage to find a short route to the East Indies, which will yield great riches for Spain.

- **Elizabeth Cady Stanton** explains why women should have the right to vote.

- **Mary McLeod Bethune** convinces people to support the school she wants to build.

- **A 19th century nurse/social worker/reformer** writes a letter-to-the-editor, or to a city council to plead for health care, nutrition, safe water, playgrounds for children, and so forth.

Nancy Smiler Levinson

Books Published:

Levinson, N. S. (1986). *I Lift My Lamp: Emma Lazarus and the Statue of Liberty.* New York: Lodestar Books, Penguin USA.

Levinson, N. S. (1988). *Clara and the Bookwagon.* New York: HarperCollins.

Levinson, N. S. (1988). *Chuck Yeager, The Man Who Broke the Sound Barrier.* New York: Walker.

Levinson, N. S. (1990). *Christopher Columbus: Voyager to the Unknown.* New York: Lodestar Books, Penguin USA.

Levinson, N. S. (1992). *Sweet Notes, Sour Notes.* New York: Lodestar Books, Penguin USA.

Levinson, N. S. (1992). *Snowshoe Thompson.* New York: HarperCollins.

Levinson, N. S. (1994). *Turn of the Century: Our Nation One Hundred Years Ago.* New York: Lodestar Books, Penguin USA.

Levinson, N. S. (1996). *Thomas Alva Edison, Great Inventor.* New York: Scholastic.

Levinson, N. S. (1997). *She's Been Working on the Railroad.* New York: Lodestar Books, Penguin USA.

Suse MacDonald

Photo by Stephen R. Swinburne

Advice for Writers:

Do what you enjoy and practice, practice, practice!

Birthplace: Evanston, IL

Education: Chatham College
University of Iowa
Radcliffe College
Art Institute
New England School of Art and Design

Enjoys: biking, tennis, gardening, and hiking

I can't remember when I first knew I was an artist, but by the time I entered college, I knew that art would be the focus of my life. In college, the courses offered were in fine arts. Commercial art was looked down upon—considered a waste of one's talents. I didn't question, I just took the courses: life drawing, painting, printmaking, and ceramics. I even made sculptures out of car parts. Nothing felt quite right. I knew I was an artist, but where did I fit?

After college, I married. My husband, Stuart, and I settled in New York City. I illustrated science text books and had a wonderful time. The studio where I worked had 30 artists, photographers, draftsmen, and even typesetters (this was before computers). I learned about and became fascinated by the commercial side of art.

Then my husband and I moved to the family farm in Weston, VT, to operate our own construction company. Our move came at a

Suse MacDonald

time when I was feeling a lack of growth in my work. I had illustrated all kinds of science books but was uncertain what to do next. So I was enthusiastic about our move and our new business. I did office work, architectural design, and drafting. We raised two children.

However, after 10 years I needed new challenges. When my second child entered first grade, I took a fast track back into illustration. I enrolled in two Boston schools: the New England School of Art and Design and the Art Institute. While in school, my focus shifted and my work became looser and more abstract. Everything I did belonged in a children's picture book.

A typography course was the catalyst for my first book. My assignment was to turn a letter of the alphabet into a representation of something. I turned an A into an owl. Afterwards I thought, if I can turn an A into an owl, why not turn A into something that begins with A. This idea led to my first book, *Alphabatics*, which won a Caldecott Honor presented by the American Library Association and the Golden Kite Award presented by the Society of Children's Book Writers.

Since then, I have done more books, mostly about transformation: taking a well-known object and turning it into something which is quite different. I love the process of writing and illustrating children's books and find real pleasure in encouraging my readers to make new connections and to see ordinary things as quite extraordinary.

Nanta's Lion by Suse MacDonald (1995)
Reprinted by permission of Morrow Junior Books
ISBN: 0-688-13125-5

Suse MacDonald

Introduction:

An alphabet exercise based on Suse MacDonald's book *Nanta's Lion* is a wonderful way to compile information and stimulate students to learn more about Africa, wild animals, and a Masaai village.

Materials:

- *Nanta's Lion* by Suse MacDonald
- Library books about Africa

Exercise:

1. Read *Nanta's Lion* aloud.

2. Discuss:

    - animals Nanta sees;
    - other animals native to Africa;
    - food chain (pages 9 & 10);
    - clues that show the passage of time; and
    - adjectives used that help describe (*favorite* grove, *thorn* trees, *two* birds, *highest termite* mound, and so forth).

3. Explain that the class will make a group alphabet book about the animals of Africa (or information about a specific topic).

4. Give each student a letter of the alphabet and have them find an animal or word beginning with that letter that has significance to Africa. There are many ways to design an alphabet book, depending on the level of your students.

Examples:

- Name an African animal and write a sentence (or paragraph) describing it.
- *A* is for Anteater. It has a long nose and mouth which it uses to hunt and eat ants and termites.

Nanta's Alphabet

- Name an African animal and describe it using alliteration. (Hairy Hyenas, Playful Parrots, Slow Sloth).

5. In pairs or small groups, have students look at other books about Africa to gather information and generate ideas about their page of the alphabet book.

6. Review their rough drafts, helping them to expand, fine tune, and focus on important elements.

7. Let each child create a finished page with illustrations. (Decide how you want the illustrations to be—collage, markers, crayons, and so forth.)

8. Bind the pages together and have students read aloud their own page to the group.

Variations:

- Have students rewrite the story, *Nanta's Lion* from another point of view. They could choose:

  - Nanta's mother;
  - the giraffe;
  - the gazelles;
  - Nanta's father;
  - the monkeys;
  - the lion; or
  - to add another character in the book—themselves perhaps?

- On a world map, locate where Nanta lives. Compare East Africa to their own area in terms of:

  - weather/climate;
  - terrain and vegetation;
  - wildlife;
  - homes;
  - clothing and jewelry; and
  - village/town or city.

Suse MacDonald

- With students, develop a Venn diagram that compares and contrasts a zoo and the African plains.

- Have students create a story wall. In small groups, students can draw/paint/collage an event from *Nanta's Lion*. Then, assemble all the event pictures in sequential order on bulletin board paper.

These lesson ideas for *Nanta's Lion* are derived from a curriculum guide by Ladene Conroy.

Published Books Written and Illustrated:

MacDonald, S. (1986) *Alphabatics*. New York: Simon & Schuster.

MacDonald, S., & Oakes, B. (1989). *Puzzlers*. New York: Scholastic.

MacDonald, S., & Oakes, B. (1994). *Sea Shapes*. New York: Harcourt Brace & Company

MacDonald, S. (1995). *Nanta's Lion*. New York: Morrow Junior Books.

MacDonald, S. (1997). *Peck, Slither and Slide*. New York: Harcourt Brace & Company.

Illustrated Books:

de Zutter, H. (1993). *Who Says a Dog Goes Bow-Wow*. New York: Doubleday Book for Young Readers.

Materials for Teachers:

Curriculum guides are available for all of the books written by Suse McDonald. For information, visit her website at http://www.create4kids.com.

Betsy Maestro

Advice for Writers:

"Good editing is as important as good writing. You should always be your own editor, first—read over your writing very carefully a number of times. Correct mistakes that you find and make sure that when someone else reads your work, they can easily understand what you've written.

After self-editing, it is essential to have someone else read your work and give you ideas about how to make it better.

Your editor can be your teacher, a parent, an older brother or sister, or someone in your class who is a good writer. Your

Photo by Saybrook Studio

Birthplace: Brooklyn, NY

Education: Southern Connecticut State University, M.S.

Enjoys: Reading and traveling.

I was born in Brooklyn, NY, and except for four years in California, I grew up in New York City in a house where books were everywhere. Naturally, I learned to love books and to love reading. I think I am really lucky to be able to earn a living writing books for kids. Although I enjoyed writing even as a child, I never imagined myself becoming a "real" writer.

My mom was a teacher, and since I liked being around kids, I decided to become a teacher, too. In New Haven, CT, at Southern Connecticut State University, I majored in early childhood education. When I graduated I got a job in East Haven, CT, teaching first grade. I continued going to school at night and earned a master's degree in counseling. After a few years, I was reassigned to a kindergarten class which I really loved, except for the part where I had to button 30 little coats in the morning and another 30 in the afternoon! My favorite time each day was story-time, when I would choose a favorite book and get to share it with my students. I know that my love of books was contagious. I like to think that I helped a lot of kids become enthusiastic readers.

Betsy Maestro

When I married Giulio Maestro, a book illustrator, I decided to try my hand at writing for young readers. I hoped that Giulio and I could work together creating books. I was delighted when one of Giulio's editors liked my idea for the re-telling of an old folktale. *A Wise Monkey Tale* was our first book together. Although it is now out of print, we still enjoy sharing it with children on our school visits.

About the same time our first book came out, our first child was born—our daughter, Daniela. It seemed the perfect time to try to work part-time at home rather than to continue teaching. By the time our second child, Marco, was born three years later, I was well on my way to a full-time writing career. Since I did not plan all this, it was a wonderful surprise to find that I could work at home at a job I loved.

In 1986, with *The Story of the Statue of Liberty*, Giulio and I began working on nonfiction. I was thrilled at the idea of creating books that would help teachers and kids in the classroom. Our *American Story* history series began with a book about the United States Constitution, called *A More Perfect Union*. We've added more titles to this series, as well as a book on American government. Other subjects we've tackled include religion, sharks, how apples grow, bats, and money. We work on so many interesting books about so many different topics that we're always learning new things. All of our books require lots and lots of research, so we do a lot of reading and visit a lot of libraries. Recently, I've begun to do some of my research on the Internet. Since we began in 1975, we've had more than 80 books published. We work for Lothrop, Lee and Shepard, Scholastic, Clarion, and HarperCollins. Nothing is more rewarding than visiting schools and seeing first-hand all of the creative ways that our books are being used in the classroom.

We live in Old Lyme, CT, along the shore between New York and Boston, in a converted barn overlooking a salt marsh. Now that our children are grown, we do more traveling—often to visit schools and libraries in other parts of the country, and also to research our latest books. Even on vacation, we visit lots of historical sights. I don't have much free time, but I always make time to read. Being a writer makes for an interesting life!

editor will see your work differently from the way you see it, so you will get a new point of view. Be willing to rewrite your story a number of times—the extra work will pay off because your story or report will be so much better.

Betsy Maestro

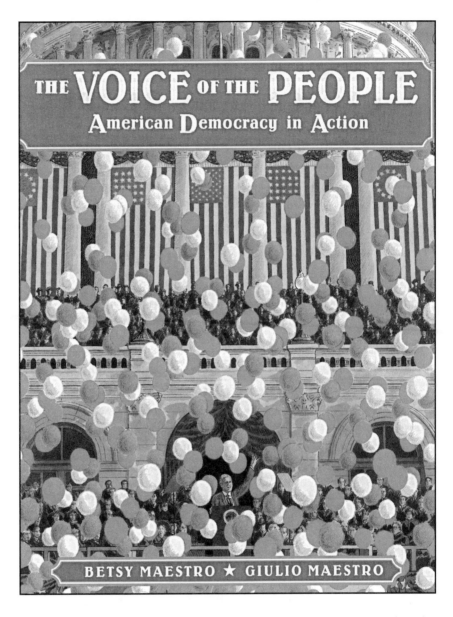

The Voice of the People: American Democracy in Action by Betsy Maestro (1996)
Illustrated by Giulio Maestro
Reprinted by Permission of Lothrop, Lee & Shepard
ISBN: 0-688-10678-1

Introduction:

Using interesting nonfiction picture books in the classroom can make science and social studies much more stimulating to students. The history series that I've worked on with my husband, illustrator Giulio Maestro, is designed to help children see that history is made up of connected events, not isolated incidents. Each book is only one chapter in the longer story of America's past, and each chapter tells the story of real people caught up in the happenings of the times, in which they lived. History is not a set of boring dates attached to remote events, rather a living, evolving story that is still being written. Everything that happened in America's past led to America's present.

Hands-on activities in the classroom enhance learning in all areas of the curriculum. If we can make history come alive for young people, they will be enthusiastic learners. Understanding history will enable students to understand our world and participate in shaping its future.

Materials:

- *The Discovery of the Americas* by Betsy Maestro.
- *Exploration and Conquest: The Americas After Columbus, 1500–1620* by Betsy Maestro.

Exercise:

1. Read *The Discovery of the Americas* and *Exploration and Conquest: The Americas After Columbus, 1500–1620* to the class.

2. After sharing these books, initiate discussion of the many explorers. Try to get your students to imagine what it must have been like to see the New World for the first time.

3. The following activities can be done individually or in pairs over a period of several days. Students should be able to work fairly independently. They may:

Bringing History to Life

Betsy Maestro

- use the two books read in class as their only references, filling in details from the imagination; or
- do additional research in the library.

4. Step-by-step instructions for your students are included after the writing activity descriptions.

I. Be a Travel Agent

1. Many explorers have returned to Europe full of fascinating stories about the New World. Ask your students to pretend they are European travel agents. Their job is to get customers to become the first tourists to visit the Americas.

2. Show students real travel brochures to help them visualize the finished product. You can get brochures at a local travel agency or send away for vacation brochures.

3. Have students study and analyze the brochures.

   - What are some of the phrases used to entice visitors?
   - What kinds of pictures are appealing?
   - Is humor used? Is there a play on words?
   - Observe different layouts, designs, and folds for the brochures.
   - Notice various kinds of lettering (bold, capitals, large print, color).
   - Discuss information given, and whether or not facts are presented in a positive manner.

4. They will prepare a fold-out brochure, with several pages, telling about the attractions of this new vacation destination. Since there are no resorts or hotels yet, they will have to come up with some innovative ideas about accommodations.

   Example: "Charming, rustic grass huts"

   - The project can be tackled in a fun and humorous way, but they must be sure to include ample factual information. A class discussion can lead students to brainstorm creative suggestions for the brochure. Guide them to think about:

- What might their customers see on this trip?
- They may describe the scenery, recreational possibilities, food, people that the tourists might encounter.
- What will these travelers need to take? (appropriate clothes, items to trade with the native people)
- What purchases might they make?
- What souvenirs would they find to take home?
- How might they communicate with the native people?
- How will they get around once they are there?
- What will the accommodations on the ship be like?

- When they have come up with the text material, they will write it in final form as it will appear in the travel brochure. Have them use exciting, colorful phrases to describe the trip in order to attract customers.

- As a final touch, they can add pictures in spots, breaking up the writing, as in a real travel folder.

II. What Did They See?

When explorers traveled across the oceans of the world, they left their friends and families behind. They were away for many months at a time and often kept diaries to record what they saw and found.

Not all explorers saw the same things or had the same experiences on their travels to the New World. For instance, Verrazano, traveling north along the Atlantic coast from the Carolinas to Maine, had a very different visual impression of the Americas from that of Francis Drake as he rounded the tip of South America and headed up the Pacific Coast.

1. Have students pretend that there is a reliable postal delivery system in place, so that they can write regular letters

Betsy Maestro

home. (Explorers sometimes did this anyway although the letters took many months to arrive in Europe.)

2.   Have each student or pair of students pick an explorer from one of the books. Have them write a letter home describing their adventures.

   - How is the temperature, weather, and climate?
   - What kinds of plants and animals have they seen? Describe some of them. (Remember, the people back home have never seen these things.)
   - What are the native people like? Describe their appearance, their dress, and so forth.
   - How does the New World compare to home? Are some things better? Some things not as good?

3.   Students can find additional information from the library.

   - Encourage them to combine some imaginative details with factual material.
   - When the students have composed their letters, have them compare the places described. If the names are kept secret, the students could guess the explorer by the description.
   - Have them illustrate their ideas to enhance the final project.

How to Work on these Activities:

1.   Discuss each activity with the class or group. Make sure they understand the goal.

2.   Each student should have a plan for working on the activity. Have them list the things they will need to do. If they are working in a group, each student should be responsible for a part of the list.

3.   Students can go to the library for additional information. Help them locate what they need, or the librarian can assist them.

4. Using the books read in class, as well as any library books, students should find the information they need. It is a good idea for them to take some informal notes or make some little pictures so that they will remember what they read.

5. Now they are ready to write. They will first write a rough draft, or working copy. They will need to read it over to correct mistakes and to make changes as needed. Then they will be ready to have it edited by their chosen editor (may be you or another student). The editor will have some suggestions on ways to improve the writing before making a final draft.

6. After all editing, the students will be ready to rewrite their story or print the edited version.

7. If they are going to do some illustrations, they will need to make a plan and a sketch first. If they work lightly in pencil, they can make changes before darkening or adding color.

8. Students may share their writing with the class. After following all of these steps, they can be proud of a job well done!

References:

Maestro, B. (1991). *The Discovery of the Americas*. New York: Lothrop, Lee & Shepard.

Maestro, B. (1994*). Exploration and Conquest: The Americas After Columbus, 1500–1620*. New York: Lothrop, Lee & Shepard.

The activities are adapted from *The Discovery of the Americas Activity Book* by Betsy Maestro. Lothrop, Lee & Shepard (1992).

Betsy Maestro

Books Published (Selected):

Maestro, B. (1981). *Traffic: A Book of Opposites*. New York: Crown.

Maestro, B. (1986). *The Story of the Statue of Liberty*. New York: Lothrop, Lee & Shepard.

Maestro, B., & Del Vecchio, E. (1987). *Big City Port*. New York: Scholastic.

Maestro, B. (1987). *A More Perfect Union: The Story of Our Constitution*. New York: Lothrop, Lee & Shepard.

Maestro, B. (1987). *Ferryboat*. New York: HarperCollins.

Maestro, B. (1989). *Snow Day*. New York: Scholastic.

Maestro, B. (1989). *Taxi: A Book of City Words*. New York: Clarion.

Maestro, B. (1990). *A Sea Full of Sharks*. New York: Scholastic.

Maestro, B. (1990). *Delivery Van: Words for Town and Country*. New York: Clarion.

Maestro, B. (1991). *The Discovery of the Americas*. New York: Lothrop, Lee & Shepard.

Maestro, B. (1992). *All Aboard Overnight: A Book of Compound Words*. New York: Clarion.

Maestro, B. (1992). *Take a Look at Snakes*. New York: Scholastic.

Maestro, B. (1992). *How Do Apples Grow?* New York: HarperCollins.

Maestro, B. (1993). *The Story of Money*. New York: Clarion.

Maestro, B. (1994). *Bats: Night Fliers*. New York: Scholastic.

Maestro, B. (1994). *Why Do Leaves Change Color?* New York: HarperCollins.

Maestro, B. (1994). *Exploration and Conquest: The Americas After Columbus 1500–1620*. New York: Lothrop, Lee & Shepard.

Maestro, B. (1996). *The Voice of the People: American Democracy in Action*. New York: Lothrop, Lee & Shepard Books.

Maestro, B. (1996). *The Story of Religion*. New York: Clarion Books.

Maestro, B. (1996). *Coming to America: The Story of Immigration*. New York: Scholastic.

Materials for Teachers:

Maestro, B. (1992). *The Discovery of the Americas Activity Book*. New York: Lothrop, Lee & Shepard.

Developing Plot
and Character

Action is character.

—F. Scott Fitzgerald

For character, too, is a process of unfolding.

—George Eliot

Judy Finchler

Photo by Jerome Finchler

Birthplace: Paterson, NJ

Education: Montclair State
Kean College

Enjoys: reading, watching "All My Children," and rooting for the New York Rangers

I consider myself so fortunate that my two careers—library media specialist and writer—are so directly related.

All day I help students learn and learn how to learn more. Some of my seventh and eighth graders even help me learn about great sites on the Internet. And nothing compares with filling a request to read *Miss Malarkey Doesn't Live in Room 10*, my own picture book. (I have 14 copies in my media center and often they're all circulating.)

Like Miss Malarkey I still consider myself a teacher and have worked in some facet of education for about 20 years, with 10 years taken off to raise my children. No, I do not live in my school library rather in a home in Parsippany, NJ. (My own library would, however, be a fun place to live with my puppets, stage, and my wonderful, wonderful books!)

I've been married for more than 30 years to Jerry, an accountant. We have a son, Todd, who practices law in Wilmington, DE, and a

Judy Finchler

daughter Lauren, who is a teacher and a future library media specialist. I also recently acquired two very special new children, Susan, Todd's wife, and Jim, Lauren's husband.

I love working with young people, especially teaching them to do research. A few years ago, I was in charge of a project where I worked on Saturdays with a group of sixth, seventh, and eighth graders researching and writing a book on Paterson, NJ (our school district) to celebrate its 200th anniversary. The book was a success and is in all the schools, libraries, public offices, and the museum.

I've always enjoyed writing from the time I was small, but it wasn't until I was well into my 40s that I attempted to sell my writing. In the first few years, I wrote and tried to sell about 20 or 25 manuscripts, with literally dozens of rejections. But persistence paid off (as it usually does) and *Miss Malarkey Doesn't Live in Room 10* became a reality.

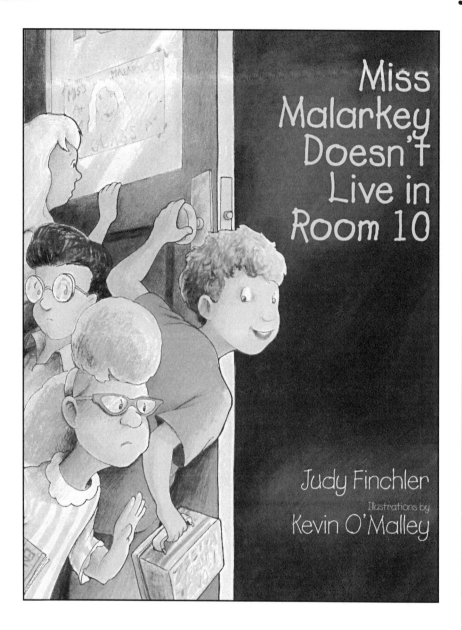

Miss Malarkey Doesn't Live in Room 10 by Judy Finchler (1995)
Illustrated by Kevin O'Malley
Reprinted by permission of Walker Publishing Co. Inc.
ISBN: 0-590-86504-8

Notable
Children's
Trade Book in
Social Studies

1995
Crayola Kids
10 Best Books

Judy Finchler

Writing Puppet Plays

Purpose:

To develop plot, characterization, and dialogue through puppet plays.

Introduction:

Writing needs to have a purpose and what better purpose is there for upper elementary children than to write and present a puppet show for the primary grades? All kinds of puppets (even the most rudimentary) come alive for youngsters. Puppets can be used in a variety of ways in the classroom. Sometimes, I use puppet plays to illustrate values (honesty, respect, responsibility, sharing, and so forth) which present lessons in a fun, but meaningful manner.

Materials:

- puppets (number and type do not matter);
- puppet stage (it can be made from a large carton); and
- picture book (to follow-up and reinforce the concept or theme from the puppet show).

Exercise:

1. Form groups of three or four students and instruct each group to brainstorm possible topics for a puppet play to present to young children.

4. The teacher circulates and guides the groups in selecting a suitable concept or idea.

2. Lessons in writing mechanics are directly related to the puppet scripts.

3. Planning and writing the plays will take several days. Teachers may break some elements into lessons which may include:

   - **Plot**—The play must be organized to include an introduction, a conclusion, and events that lead to that conclusion.

- An outline can be introduced to guide the sequence and progression of events.
- The children can "tell" their puppet show to the teacher to see if the plot works.
- Once the plot is in place, the children can easily write the script.

- **Dialogue**—Look at books to observe how characters talk.

  - Writing does not need to be full sentences. (People don't always talk in a full subject-predicate sentence.)
  - Focus on natural expressions in language.

- **Characters**—Students create a small number of characters and work on defining each character through specific traits.

  - What are some expressions the character uses?
  - What does the character like to do?
  - What makes a character angry? Sad? Happy?

- In a short puppet skit (shows should be about 5 minutes or so), characterizations are well-defined.

4. If there is an opportunity to have the groups work with another teacher (media specialist, art teacher, computer lab teacher, and so forth), make arrangements. Children sometimes work more creatively outside of the classroom.

5. When completed, the scripts can be duplicated and pasted on the back of the stage. Distribute parts, make puppets, and of course, practice.

6. Reassure students that mistakes are okay, errors are rarely obvious, and the youngsters in the audience will enjoy almost anything they see the puppets do.

Judy Finchler

Follow-up:

- I usually select a picture book to read (or have children read) as a follow-up for the puppet show.

- Select books that have similar themes as each play the groups have written.

- Keeping in mind the correlation between reading and writing, this gives the aspiring writers the chance to see what others have written.

Student Example:

Braggers Never Win
by Jose and Jayson (Sixth Grade)

Narrator: Once upon a time there was a boy named Clifford. Clifford was a pretty good basketball player. In fact, he was very good!

Clifford: (shooting baskets) I wish I were on a basketball team. Basketball is the thing!

Friend 1: Clifford, tomorrow are the tryouts for our school's team.

Clifford: What time?

Friend 1: Right after school. See you there!

Narrator: The next day after school, Clifford was the first one at the gym.

Coach: Everyone sit down on the black line. We're taking one new person for the team. Each gets three chances. Show me what you can do.

(Each player tries to make the three baskets. Clifford makes all of them.)

Coach: If you're not picked, it doesn't mean you're a bad player. You may get your chance soon. All of you have something that is good, but we can only take one.

Clifford: I know I'm going to be picked because I'm the best!

Friend 1: Well, fair is fair.

Coach: The new player is … Clifford!!!

Judy Finchler

Clifford:	(to friend 1) I told you I was the best. Out of my way! I have to get my uniform.
Narrator:	Clifford is always talking about how good he is and how much better he is than the others. He brags about himself all the time. His friends are getting annoyed with him. It is the next day at lunch.
Clifford:	(singing) I'm on the tee-team! I'm on the tee-team!
Friend 1:	(to friend 2, whispering) Get Jose.
Friend 2:	Jose! Sit by me and Jayson. (They sit down.)
Narrator:	Clifford is on the other side of the cafeteria, yet he hears them say they don't want to be his friend.
Friends:	We can't be Clifford's friend anymore because he loves himself too much. Let's make a club but Clifford isn't included.
Clifford:	Who needs them? I have the basketball team.
Narrator:	It's two months later and Clifford's team is in the playoffs. It is the last game. If they win they'll be the champions. Clifford's team members as well as the coach hate his bragging. He is not a team player. It is the last minute of the game.
Coach:	Okay, Clifford, you take it down and pass it to a teammate.
Narrator:	Clifford wants to be the hero of the game so he takes matters into his own hands and doesn't follow the coach's instructions to pass the ball. Instead he shoots! And what happens …?
Audience:	HE MISSED!
Friend 1:	I knew you were going to miss the shot.

Clifford:	Be quiet and leave me alone.
Narrator:	Clifford runs to the locker room and sits on the bench. The coach then gives him the bad news.
Coach:	You are not a team player. Hand in your uniform.
Clifford:	Good bye.
Narrator:	Three days later Clifford meets and makes up with his friends.
Clifford:	Guys, I'm sorry.
Friends:	Sorry isn't enough for the way you've been acting.
Clifford:	I know I was vain and bragged a little.
Friends:	A little!?
Clifford:	Okay, I was real vain and bragged a lot. But I won't do it any more. Can we be friends again? And can I join the club?
Narrator:	The three friends get into a huddle.
Friends:	Okay.
Narrator:	And they were friends forever!

The follow-up book we used for this play was *I'm Terrific* by Marjorie Weinman Sharmat (Holiday House).

Judy Finchler

Published and Forthcoming Books:

Finchler, J. (1995). *Miss Malarkey Doesn't Live in Room 10*. New York: Walker Publishing Co. Inc.

Finchler, J. (1998). *Miss Malarkey Won't Be in Today*. New York: Walker Publishing Co. Inc.

Emily Arnold McCully

Photo by Tom Bloom

Birthplace: Galesburg, IL

Education: Brown University
Columbia University, M.A.

Enjoys: movies and plays, reading, gardening, traveling, playing tennis, swimming, and cooking

I was born in Illinois and raised on Long Island. My father wrote for radio. Everyone in the family read voraciously. I can't remember not wanting to be a writer myself. As a small child I drew pictures that were illustrations of my favorite stories. I also wrote my own stories and illustrated them.

In school, I turned the driest assignments into "creative" exercises, illustrating reports and choosing idiosyncratic subjects that could be turned into dramas. In college, I stopped drawing and painting for the most part because there didn't seem to be enough time for everything. I loved studying and got involved in theater, acting, and writing plays. It is clear now that this was good practice for creating picture books. Every book is like a little movie or play—I cast it, make sets, costumes, then direct the scenes and play the parts in my imagination.

I am a full time writer/illustrator. My two sons are grown. Everything I admire influences my writing. I still read all of the

Advice for Writers:

"I recommend writing for a certain length of time and aiming for a goal of _X_ pages during that time. If you are vague about this, you may not produce very much. The important thing is to get stuff down on paper—then it can be shaped and worked on. The beginning stages are _not_ the time to be critical."

Emily Arnold McCully

time. I choose historical themes whenever I can for my picture books because I love doing the research. It also seems important to help teach about the past.

The most difficult part of writing is getting started. I enjoy revising, once the first draft is done—and rewrite many, many times. I try to write in the morning. I do so for four to five hours. I can draw up to eight hours at a time when working on a finished picture for a deadline. But this leads to lots of mistakes!

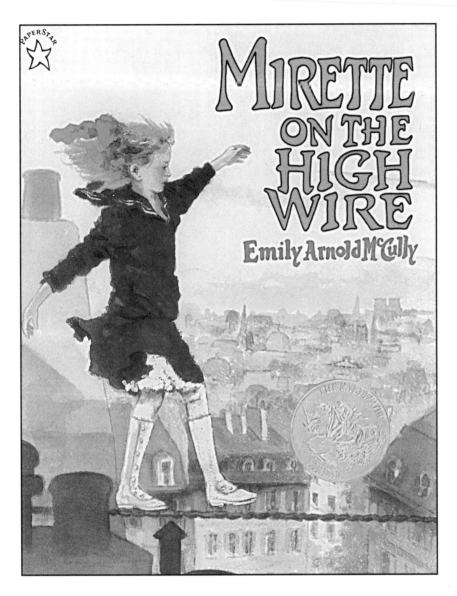

Mirette on the High Wire by Emily Arnold McCully (1992)
Reprinted by permission of Putnam
ISBN: 0-698-11443-4

Randolph
Caldecott
Medal

New York
Times Best
Illustrated
Books of the
Year

Emily Arnold McCully

Making Things Happen

Purpose:

To explore how writers make things happen in stories by making choices of plots, characters, and setting.

Introduction:

People often ask me where I get my ideas. My answer is that where they come from doesn't matter as much as where they GO. Ideas are just hints and can pop out of everyday life from memory, books, chance remarks, and so forth. They are usually tiny and fragile and must be enlarged and shaped to become full-fledged stories. A writer must be alert to ideas in order to recognize them—"Chance favors the prepared mind," Louis Pasteur said. It is useful to remember that creativity is the same for scientists and for artists.

It is also said that there are only a handful of plots. How a story is told makes it original. A writer is an observer. No one else will observe life in quite the same way or draw the same conclusions. Your ideas will be interesting because they are unlike anyone else's. A writer is also a kind of god and must not hesitate to push his or her characters around. Be bold and even crazy, as long as the story makes sense on its own terms. To test the sense of a story, I find myself asking a series of questions of my ideas. The answers, strung together, constitute the story. The answers must be chosen from any number of possibilities. Any creative endeavor is a series of choices.

The Writing Process: Making Choices

A very simple example of making choices is my wordless book *Picnic* (which, by the way, was my breakthrough). I was an illustrator for many years, working on other peoples' stories until I worked out the plot of *Picnic* and realized that it didn't need words. Somehow, the process freed me. Then, writing stories with words came more easily.

One day, I admired a red pickup truck. A little vision came to me as I sketched it: a mouse tumbling out of the back. The image was striking, so I began asking questions: who was the mouse? As it happened, I knew—I had, years earlier, made up a mouse family for a book of simple piano lessons. Next, I asked who might be driving the truck and decided to go for the obvious: the little mouse's parents were driving. Then I added grandparents, all in the cab. This mouse family, like most, would include lots of children. They were riding in the back of the truck. Where were they all going? It was a nice day, so I thought of a picnic. Clearly, they could be going anywhere, so this was a very arbitrary and conventional choice. But it left me free to explore the activities of a picnic. Every choice leads somewhere in storytelling, so you have to look ahead as well as back.

Then, I made the crucial choice: instead of placing the children so that they faced the rear of the truck, where they would see the littlest mouse fall, (and stop the truck, as well as the story), I sat them facing front so they could not see the mouse fall. Thus, the family drove on, blithely unaware they had lost someone. The little mouse was now abandoned and must cope. There were two plots established—one about the family picnic and its disruption when the loss was discovered and the other about the lost mouse.

Stories don't have to start at the beginning. My vision of the falling mouse came about a third of the way through this story. An idea can be developed with questions at any point and the story moves backward and forward. The key is to make one choice, then another, then another, with each one making the next thing happen.

Exercise 1:

1.   An exercise using pictures (which do the work of storytelling in a picture book), might be to pick a character: a cat, say, then decide how it feels, since emotions are the way characters respond to situations.

2.   Then put the cat (or animal character) into a setting: a house, a forest, a town, a yard, a spaceship, a garbage dump—whatever strikes your fancy.

3.   Next, add another character doing something to cause the cat to react.

Emily Arnold McCully

4. Try to introduce something that will change it all—say the frantic cat is treed by a ferocious dog growling below. What could come along to change the scene and keep a story going?

Exercise 2:

1. Stories about one's personal life are often the best because they matter more to the writer. Write about a time you believed your friend or a family member let you down or made you terribly angry.

2. Describe the situation: how you felt, why you thought the friend had disappointed you.

3. Then develop an ending that makes everything all right. It was just a misunderstanding; how did it happen?

4. Again, there are all kinds of possibilities. You have to choose one after the other, making sure they are logical in the story's terms. That is, in real life, people don't read other people's minds or have wings or superhuman strength. Clearing up a misunderstanding takes work, patience, and luck, not magic. Try to make up a story with a real life hero, who figures her way out of a jam—with wit, not force.

Emily Arnold McCully

Published Books Written and Illustrated:

McCully, E. A. (1985). *Picnic.* New York: Harper.

McCully, E. A. (1986). *First Snow.* New York: Harper.

McCully, E. A. (1987). *New Baby.* New York: Harper.

McCully, E. A. (1987). *The Show Must Go On.* Racine, WI: Western.

McCully, E. A. (1988). *You Lucky Duck!* Racine, WI: Western.

McCully, E. A. (1988). *School.* New York: Harper.

McCully, E. A. (1989). *Zaza's Big Break.* New York: Harper.

McCully, E. A. (1990). *The Christmas Gift.* New York: Harper.

McCully, E. A. (1990). *The Evil Spell.* New York: Harper.

McCully, E. A. (1990). *The Grandma Mixup.* New York: Harper.

McCully, E. A. (1991). *Speak Up, Blanche!* New York: Harper.

McCully, E. A. (1991). *Grandmas at the Lake.* New York: Harper.

McCully, E. A. (1992). *Mirette on the High Wire.* New York: Putnam.

McCully, E. A. (1993). *Grandmas at Bat.* New York: Harper.

McCully, E. A. (1993). *The Amazing Felix.* New York: Putnam.

McCully, E. A. (1994). *Crossing the New Bridge.* New York: Putnam.

McCully, E. A. (1994). *My Real Family.* New York: Harcourt Brace.

McCully, E. A. (1995). *Little Kit or The Industrious Flea Circus Girl.* New York: Dial Books.

McCully, E. A. (1995). *The Pirate Queen.* New York: Putnam.

McCully, E. A. (1996). *The Bobbin Girl.* New York: Dial.

McCully, E. A. (1996). *Mirette and Bellini.* New York: Putnam.

McCully, E. A. (1996). *The Ballot Box Battle.* New York: Knopf.

McCully, E. A. (1997). *Popcorn at the Palace.* New York: Harcourt Brace & Company.

Illustrated (Selected):

Bedard, M. (1997). *The Divide.* New York: Doubleday.

Byars, B. (1990). *Go and Hush the Baby.* New York: Viking.

Fox, P. (1993). *Amzat and His Brothers.* New York: Orchard Books.

Giff, P. R. (1992). *Lincoln Lions Band* (series). New York: Dell.

Gormley, B. (1981). *Mail Order Wings* (and many subsequent works). New York: Dutton.

Hall, D. (1996). *Old Home Day.* New York: Harcourt.

Emily Arnold McCully

Martin, A. (1996). *Leo the Magnificat*. New York: Scholastic.

O'Conner, J. (1986). *Lulu and the Witch Baby* and *Lulu Goes to Witch School*. New York: Harper.

O'Conner, J. (1987). *Molly* (and series). New York: Simon and Schuster.

Plath, S. (1976). *The Bed Book*. New York: Harper.

Rappaport, D. (1988). *The Boston Coffee Party*. New York: Harper.

Rockwell, T. (1973). *How to Eat Fried Worms*. Watts.

Singer, M. (1992). *In My Tent*. New York: Macmillan.

Smart, C. (1984). *For I Will Consider My Cat Jeoffry*. New York: Atheneum.

Sonneborn, R. (1970). *Friday Night is Papa Night*. New York: Viking.

Stolz, M. (1985). *The Explorer of Barkham Street*. New York: Harper.

Paul Brett Johnson

Photo by P. B. Johnson

Birthplace: Mousie, KY

Education: University of Kentucky, M.A.

Enjoys: traveling

Paul talks about how growing up in the southern mountains of eastern Kentucky has played a role in both his writing and his art. "Kentucky has a lot of towns with funny names. Take my hometown, for example, Mousie. Mousie is, as you might expect, very small. However, it was not named for its demographics. Mousie is namesake for Miss Mousie Martin, the first postmaster's daughter and sister to Miss Kitty Martin.

"Mousie lies in the heart of the Appalachian Mountains. Here I grew up alongside coal trains, annual hog killings, Sunday dinners-on-the-ground, and a whole lot of whittling and spitting. Long summer days were often spent with my grandfather, helping him to tend to his honeybees and listening to his doubtful tales.

"I began to draw and paint early on. With sketchbook in hand, I spent many an afternoon sprawled on a grassy bank drawing and dreaming. My parents were very supportive of my special interest and saw to it that I received private art lessons.

Paul Brett Johnson

"I attended the University of Kentucky and earned degrees in art and education. After teaching art in Miami, it did not take long to discover that teaching was not my calling. I moved back to Kentucky and began a string of short-lived jobs, including graphics artist for a theater group, designer and artist for a display company, freelance photographer, and illustrator of educational booklets for a state agency. In 1974 I decided it was time to devote my full energies to producing my own work. Since then I have maintained a studio in my home.

"My interest in writing and illustrating picture books first surfaced at the university. Just for fun, I had elected to take a class in children's literature. I soon found myself enthralled, and I wrote and illustrated a story of my own. Looking back, I see that it was rather awful. Nonetheless, a seed had been planted. Finally, I decided to make it happen. I did my homework. I read every how-to article and book I could find. I wrote to publishing houses for catalogues and guidelines. I spent endless hours at the library in the picture-book section. When I sat down to write, I remembered a story I had written perhaps 10 years ago but had discarded along the way. The story took place in a rural setting, which I knew well, and drew upon the tall-tale humor of a folk heritage that was my own. It seemed to have the elements of a good story—inventiveness, humor, action, and believable characters. So I rewrote the story from memory. Less than a year later, *The Cow Who Wouldn't Come Down* found its publisher, Orchard Books."

Farmer's Market by Paul Brett Johnson (1997)
Reprinted by permission of Orchard Books
ISBN: 0-531-30014-5

Paul Brett Johnson

Thinking Visually

Purpose:

To explore the process of writing by developing a simple plot structure.

Introduction:

Many writers create stories without using words at all. They are visual stories—wordless picture books. But they have a clear plot, characters, and setting.

Exercise 1:

1. Get into pairs or small teams. In the first exercise you will tell a story using only pictures, no words. You don't need to be an artist. Stick figures will do just fine.

2. Think of a story idea. You can make it up on the spot or base it on another story (don't use a familiar one) or on a real-life event. We're not going for literary excellence here, so don't be intimidated. Just come up with some ideas.

3. Divide your story into episodes—the more the merrier! Make notes if you need to, but do not write the story word-for-word.

   Example:

   1. Little Johnny gets on the school bus.
   2. Big Bob knocks Johnny's books to the floor.
   3. Johnny pulls out a … frog!

4. Now comes the fun part. It's time to think visually. Draw a picture to represent what's going on in each episode using one sheet of paper per episode (no words). It might help to think of your story as a TV program with the sound turned off. (Each episode is something that happens between commercials.)

Remember, there are no artistic merit ribbons for this exercise, so don't be ashamed of chicken-scratching. Be proud that you're creating an original story!

5.   Give your story a title and do a drawing for the title page, just a little something to pique the reader's interest. The picture could tell something about the story, to lead the reader into the book. Put all the episodes in order and staple it all together. Presto! You have just completed a wordless, picture book!

Exercise 2:

1.   In the second exercise you will write a story based on the illustrations that someone else has created.

2.   Exchange books with another team. On a clean piece of paper, write the words that could go with the other team's book.

3.   Share the writings with the entire class.

4.   Discuss:

   •   Were the illustrators successful in getting the story across without words?
   •   In what ways did the written story differ from the original story the illustrators had in mind?
   •   What do pictures do for a story?
   •   What can words do in a story that pictures cannot? (Example: Allow us to use our imaginations about how characters and places look; picture the stories in our minds; our perceptions can change with each reading.)

Other writing ideas:

1.   Read aloud *The Cow Who Wouldn't Come Down*. Have students write another episode about Gertrude and the tractor.

2.   Have a selection of wordless picture books for children to read and then create their own stories based on the illustra-

Paul Brett Johnson

tions. After they read their stories aloud to the class, discuss how individual the stories are. What elements were similar? Even though the same books were read, different stories were written because each person chooses different words to describe people and settings and expresses the action in various ways.

Suggestions of wordless picture books:

Anno's USA by Mitsumasa Anno
Window by Jeannie Baker
Grey Lady by Molly Bang
The Snowman by Raymond Briggs
Birthday Wish by Ed Emberly
A Boy, A Dog and a Frog by Mercer Mayer
Picnic by Emily Arnold McCully
School by Emily Arnold McCully
Sunshine by Jan Ormerod
Moonlight by Jan Ormerod
Rain by Peter Spier
Deep in the Forest by Brinton Turkle
Free Fall by David Wiesner

Published and Forthcoming Books Written and Illustrated:

Johnson, P. B. (1993). *The Cow Who Wouldn't Come Down*. New York: Orchard Books.

Johnson, P. B. (1994). *Frank Fister's Hidden Talent*. New York: Orchard Books.

Johnson, P. B., & Lewis, C. (1996). *Lost*. New York: Orchard Books.

Johnson, P. B. (1997). *Farmer's Market*. New York: Orchard Books.

Johnson, P. B. (1998). *A Perfect Pork Stew*. New York: Orchard Books.

Johnson, P. B. (1999). *The Pig Who Ran a Red Light*. New York: Orchard.

Illustrated Books:

Hodges, M. (1993). *Saint Patrick and the Peddler*. New York: Orchard Books.

Lyon, G. F. (1998). *A Traveling Cat*. New York: Orchard Books.

McDonald, M. (1995). *Insects Are My Life*. New York: Orchard Books.

Seymour, T. (1997). *Too Quiet for These Old Bones*. New York: Orchard Books.

Joanne Rocklin

Advice for Writers:

" Examine your world closely. Ideas are all around you, even though they seem to arrive out of nowhere! Everything and everyone is unique enough to write about—because no one else is seeing things through your eyes, or feeling with your heart. "

Photo by Gerald Nelson

Birthplace: Montreal, Quebec, Canada

Education: McGill University
California School of Professional Psychology, M.A. and Ph.D.

Enjoys: cooking, all kinds of music, swimming, walking, reading, movies, plays, and cats

Joanne Rocklin, Ph.D., has written many books for children. She gives frequent talks to classroom and adult audiences, and has been a speaker for the Society of Children's Book Writers and Illustrators and the California Reading Association. She currently teaches a course at The Learning Annex on writing for children.

Dr. Rocklin is a licensed psychologist and former elementary school teacher. She was a participant as a writer-in-residence in the 1995 University of Southern California Writing Project, a collaborative university-school program to improve student writing and the teaching of writing in the classroom.

Joanne says, "As soon as I learned to hold a pencil I began writing poems, stories, and diaries. I loved reading my own stories and library books to my two younger sisters. I have always lived within walking distance of a library. I love to read and write, but I also love to talk—especially about writing!"

Joanne Rocklin

Originally from Montreal, Canada, Joanne has two grown sons and lives in Los Angeles, CA, with her husband, Gerry, and three cats.

Joanne Rocklin

For YOUR Eyes Only! by Joanne Rocklin (1997)
Illustrations by Mark Todd
Reprinted by permission of Scholastic Press
ISBN: 0-590-67447-1

Joanne Rocklin

Purpose:

To experience how plot and character work together to create a story.

Introduction:

The purpose of this lesson is to demonstrate that plot and character can be created step-by-step as more elements are added, and especially, to demonstrate that character and plot are interrelated. Many students (of all ages) are overwhelmed by the task of plotting and characterization, not realizing that a good story has a basic, classic structure which can be utilized when writing their own.

Teachers may introduce this lesson by telling students that all writers, young and old, published or not, use some or all of the steps I've outlined. I think it would be useful to examine my novels *For YOUR Eyes Only!* or *Dear Baby*, looking for elements such as the character's problem, obstacles faced, and how the problem is solved (steps 3 through 5 in this writing exercise). Thus, an added aspect of this exercise is the development of more discerning readers, as well as writers.

Exercise:

Teachers, knowing the abilities and needs of the students best, can introduce and concentrate on one or more "steps" at a time. Another approach is to discuss the steps generally, relating them to their own lives. Some teachers work through the whole sheet orally with the students, creating the outline of a class story on the board.

These are the actual steps I use when plotting and organizing my novels. Take a look at some of the books and see if you can find the "steps."

- **Step 1: Getting started.** This gets you in the mood.

    – Loosen up—Have a snack or practice an exercise, such as:

        1. Write down three titles for a story.

Joanne Rocklin

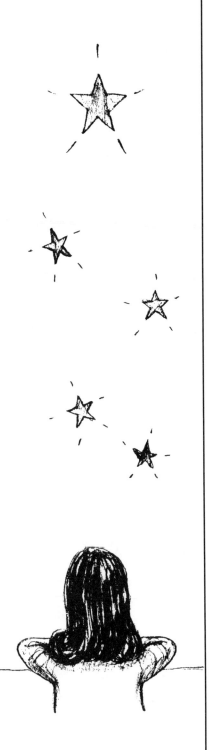

2. Finish this sentence: "I cannot write today because … " (Give three reasons.)

- _____
- _____
- _____

– Fool yourself—Pretend you will only write one or two words or sentences. Usually you end up writing more!

– Don't think!—Don't think about grades, criticism, or writing just to "get published."

- **Step 2: Brainstorming Ideas.**

1. Think about true stories from your own life. Jot down a few notes. You don't have to write a whole story at this point. Did something funny or interesting happen to you or to someone you know? Something that made you happy? Sad? Angry?

2. Think about wishes. What is your favorite wish for the future? What if it came true? Is there something you wish had happened differently in the past? You can be as imaginative as you like here!

3. Think about "What if's."

   Examples:
   – What if you were born a twin?
   – What if your family won the lottery?
   – What if you found yourself in the body of your best friend?
   – What if your favorite pet could speak?

   Now think of your own "what if's." It's fun, and it's easier than you think.

- **Step 3: Turn your idea into a story.**

1. Who is the story about? Give your character(s) a name.

2. What does your character want? Why is it so important? (If you don't know, ask him or her! Write down an imaginary conversation with your character to find out.)

3. Give your character some interesting personality traits. How do these fit in with what your character wants? (For example, Lonely? A show-off?)

4. Start your story on a day that was different for your character that relates in some way with what he or she wants.

- **Step 4: Throw rocks at your character.**

1. Have your character try at least twice to get what he or she wants, failing until the last try.

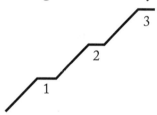

2. It's like a steep mountain that your character is climbing. It gets harder and harder to solve the problem.

- **Step 5: End your story in one of two ways:** Make sure the character has changed in some way or has learned something.

1. The character figures out how to solve the problem.

2. The problem cannot be solved, but the character gets something better.

Conclusion:

Students have enjoyed discovering that stories have a basic structure. They were able to think easily of characters' dilemmas, especially when relating them to their own lives. The realization that the character's problem does not have to be "solved," only that the character has to learn something, was extremely helpful, I have been told.

Joanne Rocklin

Books Published and Forthcoming:

Rocklin, J. (1986). *Sonia Begonia*. New York: Macmillan.

Rocklin, J. (1988). *Dear Baby*. New York: Macmillan.

Rocklin, J. (1990). *Jace the Ace*. New York: Macmillan.

Rocklin, J. (1991). *Discovering Martha*. New York: Macmillan.

Levinson, N. S., & Rocklin, J. (1992). *Feeling Great*. Alameda, CA: Hunter House.

Rocklin, J. (1993) *Musical Chairs and Dancing Bears*. New York: Holt.

Rocklin, J. (1994). *Three Smart Pals*. New York: Scholastic.

Rocklin, J. (1995). *How Much Is That Guinea Pig in the Window?* New York: Scholastic.

Rocklin, J. (1997). *The Case of the Missing Birthday Party*. New York: Scholastic.

Rocklin, J. (1997). *For YOUR Eyes Only!* New York: Scholastic.

Rocklin, J. (1997). *One Hungry Cat*. New York: Scholastic.

Rocklin, J. (1998). *Not Enough Room!* New York: Scholastic.

Rocklin, J. (1998). *The Case of the Backyard Treasure*. New York: Scholastic.

Rocklin, J. (1999). *Jake and the Copycats*. New York: Bantam Doubleday Dell.

Creating Images

The human spirit is just like a cork.

—Ernie Pyle
from WWII
Correspondences

Chapter Five

Marcia Thornton Jones

Photo by Jennifer Bearham

Birthplace: Joliet, IL

Education: Georgetown College
University of Kentucky

Enjoys: reading, going for long walks, watching movies, having fun with my husband, Steve, and our cat, Krystal

Marcia was born in Joliet, IL, and later moved to Maryland while her father worked at the Pentagon. She attended Georgetown College and University of Kentucky and is currently teaching elementary students in Lexington, KY.

According to Marcia, there is magic in the written word. "My most vivid childhood memories involve reading well-crafted stories that took me places I never imagined possible. I wanted to create magic, but no one ever taught me how to write. So my efforts were limited, and even then I felt the isolated frustration writers feel when they're not sure if their work is good.

"When I met Debbie Dadey, the librarian at the school where I taught, we talked about our mutual dream of being published authors. We said, 'What's stopping us?' We started writing during our lunch period and continued writing every day for two years with

Marcia Thornton Jones

little success. Then one day we had a rough teaching experience. It seemed as if we were invisible because of the way the students ignored us. 'What would it take to get their attention?' we asked. 'Would we have to grow eight feet tall, sprout horns, and blow smoke before they'd pay attention?' That gave us a great idea for a story.

"We wrote *Vampires Don't Wear Polka Dots*, a story about a rotten group of students who suspect their new teacher is a vampire. That book launched the best-selling series, "The Adventures of the Bailey School Kids." Since then, we've published 50 stories about the Bailey School Kids and we've developed two new series— "Triplet Trouble" and the "Bailey City Monsters" for Scholastic Inc.

"Writing is a big part of my life, now. I still don't really know how I do it, I just do it! It is full of emotions, dreams, and hopes. It challenges me to snip threads from everyday life and weave something new and colorful. Most of all, writing is just plain old fun! Once upon a time, I read books that would take me to far away, magical lands. Now I write them!"

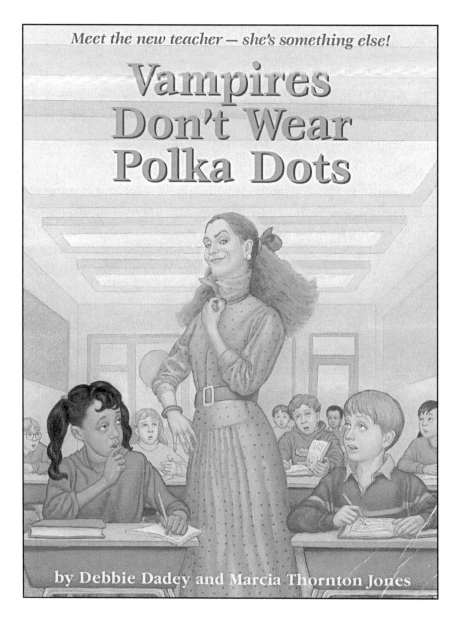

Vampires Don't Wear Polka Dots by Debbie Dadey
and Marcia Thornton Jones (1990)
Illustrated by John Steven Gurney
Reprinted by permission of Scholastic Inc.
ISBN: 0-590-43411-X

Marcia Thornton Jones

Purpose:

To create visual images, analogies, metaphors with any subject.

Introduction:

Writers often make words come alive by using images so that readers can picture in their minds what the words represent. Sometimes these visual images can be stronger when two unlike ideas are forced together. This exercise will help create memorable images by combining words in unlikely ways.

Exercise:

1. On the board, list a concept or key word from a unit you are studying.

2. Have students brainstorm ideas about the word and make a list underneath.

    Example: Write <u>Gymnast</u> on the board and have students brainstorm various words that describe what it takes to be a gymnast.

    ### <u>Gymnast</u>

balance	strength	stretching	limber
dedication	grace	discipline	rhythm
time	persistence	hard work	commitment
risk	concentration	intelligence	knowledge
practice	determination	intuition	judgment

Example: Write <u>Weather Words</u> on the board and have students brainstorm various weather words.

<u>Weather Words</u>

wind	storm	hurricane	sunny
rain	tornado	typhoon	breezy
clouds	wispy	cyclone	turbulent
hail	thunder	dark	lightning
bright	blustery	hazy	flood
dog day	wintry	spring-like	salad days

3. As a group, have students select one word (or form of the word) from the Gymnast group and one word (or form) from the Weather group and make several figures of speech.

   Examples:

   - persistence is like the wind
   - her sunny dedication
   - hazy knowledge
   - his determination was like a tornado
   - breezy rhythm
   - turbulent practice

4. Discuss a few of these images in terms of the meaning behind it.

   Example using the phrase, "His determination was like a tornado."

   - What does a tornado do? What makes it a tornado? (strength, power, destruction, stops for nothing, bounces, twirls, and so forth.)

Marcia Thornton Jones

- How could *determination* be like a *tornado*? (Doesn't let anything get in the way. Could move from one thing to another, it could be strong for a while, then die out.)

- What does this image tell us about the person? ("His determination" may indicate that he does not let anything stand in his way, he may be a bit reckless. His determination may be strong but he may bounce around from one sport to another. He may concentrate on one sport for a short time, then move on to another with equally strong commitment.)

5. Individually or in pairs, have students create other combinations of images.

6. Have them use the figures of speech in some form of writing, such as a story, paragraph, or poem.

7. Let students read their writing aloud.

8. Discuss:

   - How did specific images add to the story and make the descriptions stronger?

   - What were some images that didn't work, or that didn't present a clear picture?

   - Did some students continue the metaphor of the weather throughout the writing?

   - In what ways did the metaphors help develop a character?

Books Published:

Jones, M. T., & Dadey, D. (1990). "The Adventures of the Bailey School Kids" Series (50 books), beginning with *Vampires Don't Wear Polka Dots*. New York: Scholastic Inc.

Jones, M. T., & Dadey, D. (1995). "Triplet Trouble" Series. New York: Scholastic Inc.

Jones, M. T., & Dadey, D. (1997). "Bailey City Monsters" Series. New York: Scholastic Inc.

Selected Titles:

Jones, M. T., & Dadey, D. (1991). *Santa Claus Doesn't Mop Floors*. New York: Scholastic Inc.

Jones, M. T., & Dadey, D. (1991). *Werewolves Don't Go to Summer Camp*. New York: Scholastic Inc.

Jones, M. T., & Dadey, D. (1992). *Ghosts Don't Eat Potato Chips*. New York: Scholastic Inc.

Jones, M. T., & Dadey, D. (1992). *Leprechauns Don't Play Basketball*. New York: Scholastic Inc.

Jones, M. T., & Dadey, D. (1993). *Frankenstein Doesn't Plant Petunias*. New York: Scholastic Inc.

Jones, M. T., & Dadey, D. (1993). *Aliens Don't Wear Braces*. New York: Scholastic Inc.

Jones, M. T., & Dadey, D. (1994). *Witches Don't Do Backflips*. New York: Scholastic Inc.

Jones, M. T., & Dadey, D. (1994). *Pirates Don't Wear Pink Sunglasses*. New York: Scholastic Inc.

Jones, M. T., & Dadey, D. (1995). *Cupid Doesn't Flip Hamburgers*. New York: Scholastic Inc.

Jones, M. T., & Dadey, D. (1995). *Gremlins Don't Chew Bubble Gum*. New York: Scholastic Inc.

Jones, M. T., & Dadey, D. (1996). *Mummies Don't Coach Softball*. New York: Scholastic Inc.

Jones, M. T., & Dadey, D. (1996). *Mrs. Jeepers Is Missing*. New York: Scholastic Inc.

Jones, M. T., & Dadey, D. (1997). *Dragons Don't Cook Pizza*. New York: Scholastic Inc.

Jones, M. T., & Dadey, D. (1997). *Godzilla Ate My Homework*. New York: Scholastic Inc.

Writing Poetry

To read a poem is to hear it with our eyes;
to hear it is to see it with our ears.

—Octavio Paz

Only poetry inspires poetry.

—Ralph Waldo Emerson

Chapter Six

Celeste Lewis

Photo by B. Dennis

Birthplace: Lexington, KY

Education: University of Kentucky

Enjoys: reading, hiking, and quilting

Celeste Lewis spent her childhood on a farm, but since then she has lived in many places in the United States. She finds the people and places fascinating and educational. "I love the challenge of moving to a new place. It's a little like a clean sheet of paper that begs for a story to be written on it—it's full of possibilities."

Celeste is fortunate to get to spend a lot of time with children and see the world through their eyes. "I was read to a lot as a child, and I grew up appreciating the wide lens that children's books give the world. I've never stopped reading and collecting children's books and now I get to write them too!"

Celeste currently lives in Wyoming with her husband and two children.

Celeste Lewis

Lost by Paul Brett Johnson and Celeste Lewis (1996)
Illustrated by Paul Brett Johnson
Reprinted by permission of Orchard Books
ISBN: 0-531-09501-0

Purpose:

To produce poems from words and images that students collect from the words around them.

Exercise:

1. The first step is word gathering. This can be done by playing a game like "I Spy," where you and the students look around the room and list words that you see or hear.

    Example Words:

    *   I'm in a bookstore now, so I list the following:

postcards	shoes	cars
people	sidewalks	lights
magazines	paper bags	machines
money	windows	ceiling
books	hail	floor
noises	laughing	footsteps

2. Using the list of words, have students create spontaneous poems, surprise poems, random acts of poetry. You don't have to use all the words but try to have MOST of the entire poem come from these words only. Derivatives are fine.

    Example Poem:

    > Postcards and books fall like hailstones
    > around me.
    > I hear the noises of laughing and footsteps
    > and money clinking.
    > The sidewalks and cars change with moving people
    > This bookstore is like a window into my mind.

3. Or words from a classroom setting ...

Spontaneous Poetry

Celeste Lewis

Example:

desks	coats	books
colors	pencil	bumble bees
birds	door	leaves
trees	box	boots
window	map	

My desk is like a tight box
I try to sit still but it feels like there is no door.
A bee flies through the window
Boots scoot
    Maps flap
        Kids skid
            Coats float
We all scream and run!

Variations:

You can gather words from other sources. Some examples are listed below.

- Use the first word from every page or chapter of a book.
- Use words from a newspaper's headlines, headers on sections in a magazine, and so forth.
- Go around the group and have everyone choose one word off the top of their heads.
- "Poetry Kits" are on the market now with lots of words on small magnetic pieces. Words can be moved all around to make various poems. Children can make their own version of this game by writing words on pieces of cardboard, then swapping with each other.

4.   Students can write poems from a common list of words they generate together, or they can create individual lists. It is interesting to see the great variation of poetry that emerges from using the same word list.

There are endless possibilities for writing random poems and, therefore, endless possibilities for fun and creativity!

Book Published:

Johnson, P. B., & Lewis, C. (1996). *Lost*. New York: Orchard Books.

George Ella Lyon

Advice for Writers:

"*Write for the joy of discovery, the mystery of story, the freedom of building a world with words.*"

Photo by Linda Butler's Studio

Birthplace: Harlan, KY

Education: Center College
University of Arkansas, M.A.
Indiana University, Ph.D.

Born and raised in the mountains of Kentucky, George Ella Lyon grew up with a love for poetry and music. She wrote her first poems in second and third grade, and continued writing through high school and college. Reading and writing were cultivated by a family rich with stories and blessed with a love for literature.

She has published two collections of poems (*Mountain* and *Catalpa*, winner of the Appalachian Book of the Year award), 13 picture books (including *Come a Tide*, featured on "Reading Rainbow," *Who Came Down That Road?*, a *Publishers' Weekly* Best Book of the Year, and *Basket*, winner of the Kentucky Bluegrass Award), three novels for young readers (including *Borrowed Children*, winner of the Golden Kite Award), an autobiography (*A Wordful Child*, in the Richard Owen Meet-the-Author series), and *Choices*, a book of stories for adult new readers. Her work is featured in the new PBS series, "The United States of Poetry."

George Ella Lyon

Writing picture books was a natural evolution from George Ella's poetry. Using rhythms and sounds and imagery and surprise, her poems easily found their way into picture books. She took many cues from her own young children as they questioned, imagined, and wondered with the innocence and vulnerability of tender years.

George Ella Lyon

Mama Is a Miner by George Ella Lyon (1994)
Illustrated by Peter Catalanotto
Reprinted by permission of Orchard Books
ISBN: 0-531-06853-6

Purpose:

To create many varied images and comparisons using the five senses.

Exercise:

1. Have a basket of different types of bread or slices of various kinds of apples (or, if you prefer, use a familiar experience such as "snow" or "ocean").

2. If using food, pass around the samples along with napkins or paper towels. If using the word alone, write it in large letters on the board or flip chart.

3. Explain that because good writing speaks to us through our senses, we're going to explore this bread (or apples or ocean) with that in mind.

4. Have students name the five senses. List these on the board. Then write down their ideas of how the food or word tastes, sounds, feels, smells, and looks.

5. Direct them to make a comparison. If they just give a description, such as "snow feels cold" ask, "cold as what, what else is cold?"

    Note: With younger children, I ask them to give me their responses verbally. With an older group, I have them write their list and then pick one or two comparisons to share. Either way, we end up with a board or page full of images under each category.

6. From this point, there are several directions to go:

    •   Demonstrate how a poem could be built from these components by free-reading five or so in a quickly determined order.
    •   Let students choose whether to list (An apple tastes like …) or address the apple (Apple, you taste like …).

Coming to Your Senses

George Ella Lyon

- Then ask them to choose beginning and ending images. Let them decide whether to group by senses or just alternate.

- Either continue developing the poem as a large group with the teacher writing their images on the board, or have students use the list of ideas to develop their own poems in small groups or individually.

6. Throughout this process, discuss the advantages and disadvantages of various choices, emphasizing that there is no right or wrong choice. However, each word choice affects the poem, which students can understand by trying various words to decide which word says what they intend.

7. If there is more time or computer support, someone could type the images and print copies for students to use at a later time.

Note: This exercise is fun and playful and gives children the chance to ride the roller coaster of poem-making together. This can be tried many times with different prompts and increasing levels of student involvement.

Enjoy!

Books Published:

Lyon, G. E. (1985). *Father Time and the Day Boxes*. New York: Aladdin.

Lyon, G. E. (1986). *A Regular Rolling Noah*. New York: Aladdin.

Lyon, G. E. (1988). Borrowed Children. New York: Bantam.

Lyon, G. E. (1989). *A B Cedar: An Alphabet of Trees*. New York: Orchard Books.

Lyon, G. E. (1989). *Together*. New York: Orchard Books.

Lyon, G. E. (1990). *Come a Tide*. New York: Orchard Books.

Lyon, G. E. (1990). *Basket*. New York: Orchard Books.

Lyon, G. E. (1991). *Cecil's Story*. New York: Orchard Books.

Lyon, G. E. (1991). *The Outside Inn*. New York: Orchard Books.

Lyon, G. E. (1993). *Dreamplace*. New York: Orchard Books.

Lyon, G. E. (1994). *Mama is a Miner*. New York: Orchard Books.

Lyon, G. E. (1994). *Five Live Bongos*. New York: Scholastic.

Lyon, G. E. (1994). *Here and Then*. New York: Orchard Books.

Lyon, G. E. (1996). *Ada's Pal*. New York: Orchard Books.

Lyon, G. E. (1996). *A Day at Damp Camp*. New York: Orchard Books.

Lyon, G. E. (1996). *A Wordful Child*. Meet-the Author Series. New York: Richard C. Owen Publisher Inc.

Lyon, G. E. (1997). *The Stranger I Left Behind Me*. Mahwah, NJ: Troll Paper Back Books. Originally published as *Red Rover, Red Rover*. New York: Orchard Books (1989).

Megan McDonald

Advice for Writers:

"If you want to write ... READ!"

Photo by Michelle McDonald

Birthplace: Pittsburgh, PA

Education: Oberlin College
University of Pittsburgh, M.L.S.

Enjoys: Reading, exploring tide pools, eating ice cream, growing weird vegetables (purple beans, yellow watermelon ...) e-mailing my sisters, rubber stamping, animals I'm not allergic to, the color purple, watching thrillers, cleaning house ... NOT!

I grew up in a house full of books in Pittsburgh, PA, the youngest of five girls. My father, an ironworker, built bridges all across the city, including the real Bridge to Nowhere. Known among ironworkers as Little Johnny, he was a great storyteller. My mother, a social worker, was a very good listener. Dinnertime took place at a large round table in the kitchen, where the seven of us gathered nightly, talking and telling stories. With four older sisters, I couldn't get a word in edgewise. I'm told I began to stutter. That's when I first started writing things down.

What I remember of childhood is summer. The woods, the creek, the goldfish pond. Skinned knees from climbing in tree wells. Picking blackberries. Searching for nickels in old tree stumps, where my father used to hide them. Chasing after the ice-cream truck.

Megan McDonald

Deep down, I always wanted to be a writer. In the meantime, I've had jobs as a park ranger, chambermaid, cook, tour guide, and storyteller. I've worked in bookstores, libraries, and schools, a children's theater company, a children's museum, and a museum full of old cars and fire engines! I knew that I wanted to write books for children when I heard Richard Jackson, my editor, speak at a conference. It took me two years from that time to work up the courage to send him a manuscript. When I finally did, it got lost in the mail … twice!

Ideas are like secrets waiting to be told. An idea begins as a tiny seed, then swells inside me until it captures my imagination, makes me laugh, or strikes me deeply. Ideas come from inside out and outside in. An idea may enter with the surprising force of a thunderclap or slowly, gradually shape itself over time. The idea for my first book, *Is This a House for Hermit Crab?* grew out of a story told with puppets to children at the library. Its alliterative sounds, its rhythm and repetition worked so well with children that I imagined it as a picture book, in hopes that it might find a wider audience.

Megan McDonald

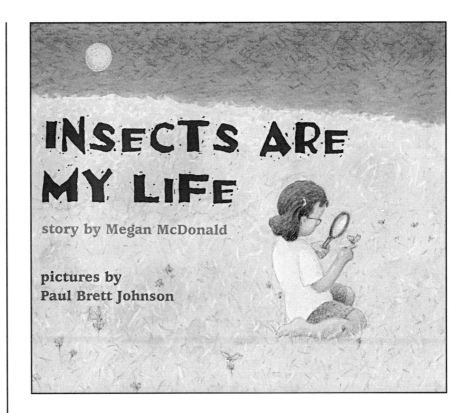

Insects are My Life by Megan McDonald (1995)
Illustrated by Paul Brett Johnson
Reprinted by permission of Orchard Books
ISBN: 0-531-06874-9

Introduction:

Kids love to solve riddles. Here's a quick and easy way to get young writers thinking in a different way, seeing with a writer's eye. Writers and non-writers alike will have fun creating a short poem based on an everyday object that uses imagery and metaphor in a guessing-game riddle that begs to be solved.

Exercise:

1. **Thinking Images**

Before introducing the idea of a riddle, talk about imagery including simile and metaphor. Read passages from books or poems you like that contain interesting images. Have students listen and think about and comment on if they like the image, if it makes sense, what it means, and what pictures it conjures in the imagination.

- When is the moon like a silver eyebrow in the sky?
- Can a person's hair really be the sawblade color of a grasshopper's wing?
- How might an angry teenager be compared to a Siamese fighting fish?

You can even have students practice by finishing a sentence:

The moon is the color of _____.
She folded her hands like _____.
The yellow leaf was a _____.

Try to stretch students beyond clichés. Everybody has heard the idea of something being as tall as a building, as soft as a feather, as high as the sky. Brainstorm together to come up with brand new images that don't fall into the same tired categories.

2. **Reading Riddle Poems Aloud**

Demonstrate by example. Sylvia Cassedy, in her book *In Your Own Words*, has a chapter on Riddle Poems with samples from

Megan McDonald

Mother Goose to Emily Dickinson. Use any good "Who Am I?" or "What Am I?" book for examples. Pull excerpts from poetry anthologies.

Younger children may enjoy the humorous *Riddle-icious* by J. Patrick Lewis or the multicultural *A Basket Full of White Eggs* by Brian Swann. Read the poems aloud, and allow children to guess.

- **Examples** from *In Your Own Words*:

A silver-scaled dragon with jaws flaming red
Sits at my elbow and toasts my bread.
     —William Jay Smith   (toaster)

I am a molting bird;
My feathers, orange and red,
drop gently to the ground.
     —Sylvia Cassedy   (tree in fall)

Thirty white horses upon a red hill.
Now they tramp, now they champ, now they stand still.
     —Mother Goose   (teeth)

Vary the writing examples you use to fit the age level. I have successfully used this exercise with kids from second grade through high school!

3. **Preparing to Write**

Begin with an everyday object, especially for those reluctant writers. Make sure children are familiar with the object. Objects can be small enough to fit in a hand. Prepare the number of objects you need for your class ahead of time by hiding them in plain envelopes. Then pass out an envelope to each individual, asking them *not* to show it to anyone. Kids love the secrecy of this. Tell them you'll want classmates to guess their riddle poems later.

- Here's a list of things to get you started:

feather	pencil	map
old key	safety pin	paper clip
Band-Aid®	postage stamp	clothespin
ribbon	rock	ball
button	bead	marble
magnifying glass	shell	crayon
shoelace	old letter	friendship bracelet

Inevitably, some students will be dissatisfied with the object. Ask them to stick to what they received. Perhaps they may choose another object later to write an additional riddle poem. If they trade, everyone may want to. Small groups work well to allow you time to "visit" with each child individually.

4. **Composing the Riddle Poem**

Ask students to take a few minutes to think about their object. Have them think about what it looks like, what it does, what it's used for, what color and size it is, what comparisons they might make. The five senses come in handy here. What is its shape, smell, texture? Does it have a taste, a sound? Prompt them to think about it in a new way, compare it to something totally dissimilar. Remind them not to give it away by telling what the object is.

5. **Editing and Rewriting**

- Students will most likely need help being more or less specific. For example, if they write, "I am big and round" there are many things which fit that description, and they will need help narrowing the object's attributes. If they write, "Play catch with me by bouncing me on the sidewalk" they've revealed that their object is a ball. A riddle poem is like a hint, a secret half told. There must remain an element of mystery.

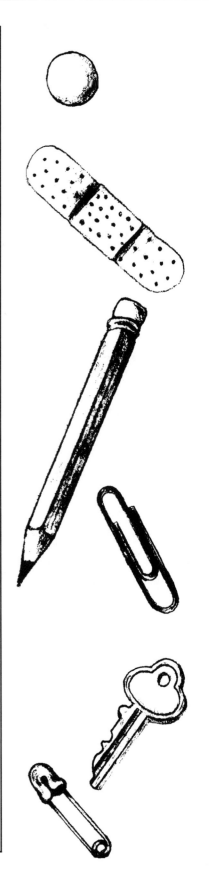

Megan McDonald

- Ask yourself, "Is there anything else that fits my description?" For example, if the object fits in a pocket, and can be used to hold a marble, a wad of already-chewed gum or as the bed of a cricket, can you think of other things it may be besides a matchbox? If so, listeners will need another clue.

- Once students have their basic composition, they may also need help shaping it into a poem. A riddle poem does not have to begin with "I am" and end with "What am I?" and it does not have to rhyme. But it does have to use language well, so that it sounds like poetry!

6. **Variations on a Theme**

- Extend this activity by having students use an animal or something from nature or even their own hand as their subject. Imagination's the limit!

- Use a magnifying glass or jeweler's loupe to look at the object up close, to literally see it in a different way. What comparisons can you make now that weren't thought of before?

- Create a group poem. Choose a topic or object and combine images given by the whole class into a single poem.

7. **I'm Done!**

Have fun sharing the completed poems aloud while class members try to guess the riddles. You'll find that kids have great enthusiasm for this! By the time you're finished, kids will have worked on developing thinking skills by analogy, problem solving, creativity, powers of observation. Given a chance, they never fail to come up with rich, unusual, imaginative, surprising images!

Megan McDonald

Books Published

McDonald, M. (1990). *Is This a House for Hermit Crab?* New York: Orchard Books.

McDonald, M. (1991). *The Potato Man.* New York: Orchard Books.

McDonald, M. (1992). *The Great Pumpkin Switch.* New York: Orchard Books.

McDonald, M. (1992). *Who-oo Is It?* New York: Orchard Books.

McDonald, M. (1993). *The Bridge to Nowhere.* New York: Orchard Books.

McDonald, M. (1995). *Insects Are My Life.* New York: Orchard Books.

McDonald, M. (1996). *My House Has Stars.* New York: Orchard Books.

McDonald, M. (1997). *Tundra Mouse*: *A Storyknife Tale.* New York: Orchard Books.

McDonald, M. (1997). *Beezy.* New York: Orchard Books.

References:

Cassedy, S. (1979). *In Your Own Words.* Garden City: Doubleday.

Lewis, J. P. (1996). *Riddle-icious.* New York: Knopf.

Swann, B. (1988). *A Basket Full of White Eggs.* New York: Orchard Books.

Naomi Shihab Nye

Photo by Bessie Loeppert

Birthplace: St. Louis, MO

Education: Trinity University

Enjoys: reading, cooking, bicycling, traveling, and collecting old postcards

We go back and back, to where it all begins. The sources, the mysterious wells. Each thing gives us something else.

It wasn't whether you were rich or poor, but if you had a big life, that's what mattered. A big life could be either a wide one or a deep one. It held countless possible corners and conversations. A big life didn't stop at the alley or even the next street. It came from somewhere and was going somewhere, but the word *better* had no relation, really. A big life was interesting and wore questions easily. A big life never, for one second, thought it was the only life.

Something was in the closet, besides our clothes, which might or might not be friendly. A branch scratched a curious rhythm on the dark window. I told my brother it was talking to us. Our father came from Palestine, a beloved land across the sea. Some people call it the Holy Land. Both my parents seemed holy to me. At night our father sat by our beds, curling funny stories into the air. His musical talking stitched us to places we had not been yet. And our mother, who had grown up in St. Louis, where we were growing up, floated us to sleep on a river of songs: "Now rest beneath night's shadow …" She had been to art school and knew how to paint people the way they looked on the inside, not just the outside. That's what I wanted to know about, too. What stories and secrets did people carry with them? What songs did they hold close inside their ears?

Reading cracked the universe wide open—suddenly I had the power to understand newspapers, menus, books. I loved old signs, Margaret Wise Brown, Louisa May Alcott, Carl Sandburg, the exuberant bounce of sentences across the page. I remember shaping a single word—*city*, *head*—with enormous tenderness. In second grade my class memorized William Blake's "Songs of Innocence." Reading gave us voices of friends speaking from everywhere, so it followed that one might write down messages, too. Already I wrote to find out what I knew, and what connected. Sometimes writing felt like a thank you note, a response to what had already been given.

My German-American grandmother gave me a powder puff, which, when tapped 30 years later, still emits a small, mysterious cloud.

My Palestinian grandmother gave me a laugh and a tilt of the head.

My great-uncle Paul gave me a complete sewing kit 100 years old and one inch tall.

Whenever people have asked, "Where do you get ideas to write about?" I wonder, "Where do you *not*?"

My family moved to Jerusalem (Jordan, then) when I was 14, to live near our Arab relatives for a year. Later we came to Texas, where neither of my parents had any history at all. Texas embraced us. There was so much room we could fit into. Libraries still felt like sanctuaries. I could name so many "favorite writers" of any era of my life—Henry David Thoreau got me through high school and Jack Kerouac through college. The poems of William Stafford have deepened my life since I was 15. The poems of W.S. Merwin give

Remember, too much praise can be as paralyzing as too much criticism. Don't worry if your family acts neutral to what you write. That can almost be better sometimes.

Identify yourself as a writing person to other people! You will then be surprised how many other writers materialize around you.

Be lavish and abundant with your words—paper is cheap. Let yourself go in first drafts and learn to come back to your writing with a calmer, more careful editing eye.

The door will open wide if you let it!

Naomi Shihab Nye

me daily inspiration. The poems of contemporary women say, *You will never be alone!* I used to spend hours in libraries devouring literary journals; that sense of wealth and variety stays with me. I feel slightly suspicious of writers who say they don't read much.

Now I live with my husband, photographer Michael Nye, and our son, Madison, who likes computers, weather radios, and electrical inventions, as well as books. We have been reading together since he was born. We share an old home one block from the quiet little San Antonio River, downtown. I want to dig under our house. My poems and stories often begin with the voices of our neighbors, mostly Mexican-American, always inventive and surprising. I never get tired of mixtures.

Working as a visiting writer in schools for more than two decades all around Texas, and in Oregon, Hawaii, and Alaska, among other places, I have collected poems by writers everywhere to share with students.

This Same Sky: A Collection of Poems from Around the World
Selected by Naomi Shihab Nye (1992)
Reprinted by permission of Deborah Maverick Kelley
Four Winds Press
ISBN: 0-02-768440-7

ALA
Notable
Children's
Award

Booklist
Editor's
Choice Award

Naomi Shihab Nye

Purposes:

To think in metaphor about ourselves as unique individuals. To experience the connections between food and writing and life.

Exercise 1:

1. Read a poem or two to the class that describes or wonders about one's own identity. Then tell the students you're going to give them a "quiz" they can't possibly fail. They may write an answer with a word, phrase, or sentence. The only rule is, they cannot answer the same way twice.

2. Ask them 10 times in a row (emphasizing the question differently):

   - "WHO are you?"
   - "Who ARE you?"
   - "Who are YOU?"
   - Or sometimes I vary this, asking them 5 times, "Who are you?" and 5 times, "Where do you come from?"

   They will laugh; they will protest; they will write.

3. Ask for volunteers to read their lists. Invariably, somebody (I hope) will have used metaphor instead of fact:

   - I am a planet spinning in space.
   - I am a thin wisp of disappearing wind.
   - I am a lost and lonely dog.

4. If not, YOU suggest metaphor as a way one might have answered, to extend the possibilities. (See the following poem by Scott Momaday which does this.)

5. Then talk about how poetry is a continual consideration and exploration of identities—who we are and aren't, how we do and don't fit together, as human beings, friends, and so forth. Talk about this in whatever ways you want. Read

some poems from various traditions which examine our changing identity. (See examples.) Talk about how the question is never answered once and for all. Who did we used to be? Who will we be tomorrow? Write some provocative questions and sample metaphors on the board. (Metaphor is contagious pleasure! The more it's seen, the more it happens.)

6. Invite them to write some identity poems of their own. Take about 10 minutes for this. Ask for some to share. Or, you may collect a few and read anonymously.

Naomi Shihab Nye

The Delight Song of Tsoai-Talee

I am a feather on the bright sky.
I am the blue horse that runs in the plain.
I am the fish that rolls, shining, in the water.
I am the shadow that follows a child.
I am the evening light, the lustre of meadows.
I am an eagle playing with the wind.
I am a cluster of bright beads.
I am the farthest star.
I am the cold of the dawn.
I am the roaring of the rain.
I am the glitter on the crust of the snow.
I am the long track of the moon in a lake.
I am a flame of four colors.
I am a deer standing away in the dusk.
I am a field of sumac and the pomme blanche.
I am an angle of geese in the winter sky.
I am the hunger of a young wolf.
I am the whole dream of these things.

You see, I am alive, I am alive.
I stand in good relation to the Earth.
I stand in good relation to the gods.
I stand in good relation to all that is beautiful.
I stand in good relation to the daughter of Tsen-tainte.
You see, I am alive, I am alive.

—N. Scott Momaday

Momaday, N. S. (1974). *Angle of Geese and Other Poems*. Boston: David R. Godine.

Naomi Shihab Nye

Poetry Examples—Identity

Chicago Poet

I saluted a nobody.
I saw him in a looking-glass.
He smiled—so did I.
He crumpled the skin on his forehead,
Frowning—so did I.
Everything I did he did.
I said, "Hello, I know you."
And I was a liar to say so.

Ah, this looking-glass man!
Liar, fool, dreamer, play-actor,
Soldier, dusty drinker of dust—
Ah! he will go with me
Down the dark stairway
When nobody else is looking,
When everybody else is gone.

He locks his elbow in mine,
I lose all—but not him.

—Carl Sandburg

Sandburg, C. (1950). *Complete Poems*. New York: Harcourt Brace.

Naomi Shihab Nye

I'm Alone

I am alone.

My sister was playing baseball.
My dog was chewing a big bone
My three brothers were fighting
I got into the fight,
But I end up crying.

I had 10 dollars in my sock.
My mother washed the sock.

I was riding my bike
And the chain busted.
I went home and fixed it.
I went to the gas station
To put some air in my tire
But it exploded.

I don't do anything.
I'm all alone.

Alex Huerta
Grade 2
San Antonio, TX

Naomi Shihab Nye

Student Examples—Identity

Who Am I?

I am my Mother,
Her expectations of me,
Her thoughts of me.
She always says that I am smarter
Than she was in school.
She says she is proud of me.
I try to make her proud.
I try to be what she sees in me.

I am the pleaser of the people
Who know me.
    I am each person's idea
Of me. I try to be
    what they see in me.

I try to please everyone.
    It is hard.
I have a conflict inside me.
Should I be what I want to be
    or what they see in me?
Should I be me
    or each person's mirror of me?
I try to have my own beliefs,
    but respect others' beliefs.

It is hard to be me!

David Collins
Grade 8
Mars Hill, ME

Naomi Shihab Nye

Untitled

I feel like a snowflake going where
He wants. Going very slow and peaceful. I feel
Like a bear cub emerging from a long sleep.
I feel like a flower blossoming into the sun.

I feel like a cat after it's been scratched.
I feel like a dog after it's seen its master
For the first time. Like a violin after it's been
Tuned. Like a song after it's been sung. Like
A rose with a beautiful bud. Like a horse
With a newborn colt. Like a country that just
Won a war.

> Robert Andrews
> San Antonio, TX

A Horse with Wings

I'm a horse with wings.
I'm flying through the air.
I'm beautiful when I spread my wings out.

I'm beautiful when I fly.
I'm a white stallion on a mountain.
I'm a hundred horses put together.

> Ray Martinez
> Grade 4
> San Antonio, TX

Naomi Shihab Nye

Student Examples—Identity

Untitled

Hours are leaves for me
And I am their gardener ...
Each hour falls down slow.

> Susan Morrison
> Australia

Naomi Shihab Nye

Exercise 2:

1. I carry a big straw basket full of mixed fruits and vegetables into a classroom and line them on the table. I have the students name each one and let somebody write all the names onto the board. Purposely, I include many common samples and some exoticas.

2. Then I ask a series of questions about the fruits and vegetables:

   - Which are your favorites?
   - Which have you never tasted?
   - Which one reminds you most of your father? Your grandfather?

   … and any other questions that might focus on details, qualities, and characteristics. If possible, slice some open for viewing, smelling, and tasting.

3. Ask students to write a series of sensory sentences, such as:

   • The skin of the avocado feels like _____.
   • The seeds of the kiwi look like _____.

4. Discuss how fruits and vegetables, the tangible delicacies of the world, are intricately connected with memory. I always tell stories—how I could never eat a slice of cantaloupe without thinking of my mother's mother and why. I like the fact that one may mix scientific and descriptive data easily here. We talk about everything from recipes to pesticides, all in the name and spirit of poetry!

5. Students can develop the sensory sentences and food stories into poems and share with the group.

This writing idea has never failed to elicit some truly wonderful student poems. A girl named Pearl wrote a poem comparing herself to "pearl onions." A boy wrote about wanting to float away in a kiwi boat. They would write, read, and try things they'd never tasted. Somehow this spirit of eating and appetite was crucial to the spirit of writing, too. Everything connected—all the words and tastes. Stem. Ground. Harvest. Meal.

Cheers!

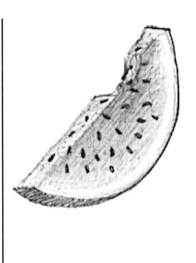

Naomi Shihab Nye

Poetry Examples—Fruits & Vegetables

Fiesta Melons
In Benidorm there are melons,
Whole donkey-carts full

Of innumerable melons,
Oval and balls,

Bright green and thumpable
Laced over with stripes

Of turtle-dark green.
Choose an egg-shape, a world-shape,

Bowl one homeward to taste
In the whitehot noon:

Cream-smooth honeydews,
Pink-pulped whoppers,

Bump-rinded cantaloupes
With orange cores.

Each wedge wears a studding
Of blanched seeds or black seeds

To strew like confetti
Under the feet of

This market of melon-eating
Fiesta-goers.

—Sylvia Plath

Hughes, T. (Ed.). (1981). *The Collected Poems of Sylvia Plath*. New York: Harper & Row, Publishers.

Naomi Shihab Nye

Poetry Examples—Fruits & Vegetables

Summer's Bounty

berries of Straw   nuts of Brazil
berries of Goose   nuts of Monkey
berries of Huckle   nuts of Pecan
berries of Dew   nuts of Grape

berries of Boisen   beans of Lima
berries of Black   beans of French
berries of Rasp   beans of Coffee
berries of Blue   beans of Black

berries of Mul   beans of Jumping
berries of Cran   beans of Jelly
berries of Elder   beans of Green
berries of Haw   beans of Soy

apples of Crab   melons of Water
apples of May   melons of Musk
apples of Pine   cherries of Pie
apples of Love   cherries of Choke

nuts of Pea   glories of Morning
nuts of Wal   rooms of Mush
nuts of Hazel   days of Dog
nuts of Chest   puppies of Hush

—May Swenson

Swenson, M. (1994). *Nature: Poems Old and New*. New York: Houghton Mifflin Company.

Naomi Shihab Nye

Poetry Examples—Fruits & Vegetables

Ajo, Cebolla y Chile Roja
(garlic, onion, & red chile)

On certain summer days
breaking out in a
mopping/scrubbing/washing kinda sweat
I catch that hint of my mother
floating around

My head drops
back into her lap
where my braids were tugged into place
that hint of my mother
mixing with the ajo, cebolla, y chile rojo

On certain summer days
breaking out in a certain sweat
I can't tell if it's me
or if it's her essence
that she braided into my hair.

—Maria S. Limòn

Dunning, S., Lueders, E., Nye, N., Gilyard, K., & Worley, D. (Eds.). (1995). *Reflections on a Gift of Watermelon Pickle* (2nd ed.). Glenview, IL: Scott Foresman.

Naomi Shihab Nye

Books Published (Selected):

Nye, N. S. (Ed.). (1992). *This Same Sky: A Collection of Poems from Around the World*. New York: Simon & Schuster Books for Young Readers.

Nye, N. S. (1994). *Sitti's Secrets*. New York: Maxwell Macmillan International.

Nye, N. S. (1994). *Red Suitcase*. Brockport, New York: BOA Editions Ltd.

Nye, N. S. (1995). *Benito's Dream Bottle*. New York: Simon & Schuster Books for Young Readers.

Nye, N. S. (Ed.). (1995). *The Tree Is Older Than You Are: A Bilingual Gathering of Poems & Stories from Mexico*. New York: Simon & Schuster Books for Young Readers.

Nye, N. S. (1995). *Words Under the Words: Selected Poems*. Portland, OR: Far Corner Books/Eighth Mountain Press.

Nye, N. S. & Janeczko, P. B. (Eds.). (1996). *I Feel A Little Jumpy Around You: A Book of Her Poems & His Poems Presented in Pairs*. New York: Simon & Schuster.

Nye, N. S. (1997). *Never in a Hurry: Essays on People and Places*. Columbia, SC: University of South Carolina Press.

Nye, N. S. (1997). *Lullaby Raft*. New York: Simon & Schuster.

Nye, N. S. (1997). *Habibi*. New York: Simon & Schuster.

A Guggenheim Fellow for 1997–98, Naomi has traveled abroad on three *Arts America* speaking tours and is featured in two PBS poetry programs, "The Language of Life with Bill Moyers" and "The United States of Poetry."

Editing

The difference between the right word and the nearly right word is the same as that between lightning and the lightning bug.

—Mark Twain

Chapter Seven

Robert Munsch

Photo by R. Munsch

Birthplace: Pittsburgh, PA

Education: Studied for Roman Catholic priesthood for 7 years
Fordham University
Boston University, M.A.
Tufts University, M.Ed.

Enjoys: cycling and geology

A natural-born storyteller, Robert Munsch has entertained and delighted thousands of children, teachers, and parents for more than 20 years. He usually tells a story many times to audiences before he puts it into words in a book.

The protagonists in Munsch's books are typically spirited children who challenge conventions, progress through various hilarious steps, then somehow find simple solutions.

Born in Pittsburgh, PA, Munsch immigrated to Canada. His background includes anthropology and child studies at Boston University and Tufts University, respectively. He has been a teacher, professor, and a performing artist as well as a prolific writer. Many of his best-loved stories have been made into audio recordings with Munsch telling his own lively tales. Robert's books have been translated into nine languages, including Spanish, French, German, and Swedish.

Robert Munsch

Love You Forever by Robert Munsch (1987)
Illustrated by Sheila McGraw
Reprinted by permission of Firefly Books Ltd.
ISBN # 0-920668-36-4

Purpose:

To edit and fine tune our stories naturally through storytelling.

Exercise:

1. Choose something that you already tell people. It probably starts with, "Well, once I ..." or "Did I ever tell you about the time ..." It does not have to be true, just something you tell as if it were true.

    *   OK—got one?
    *   Good.

2. What you have is a story—a tell story. Don't write it down and don't memorize it.

3. Over the next two days tell it to five different people and have fun telling it better and better.

    *   Done that?
    *   Great. You just edited your story five times.

4. Now write it down. Done.

5. If you think it is really good, keep telling it and then write it down again at a later time.

Automatic Editing

Robert Munsch

Books Published:

Munsch, R. (1979). *The Dark*. Toronto: Annick Press.

Munsch, R. (1979). *Mud Puddle*. Toronto: Annick Press.

Munsch, R. (1980). *The Paper Bag Princess*. Toronto: Annick Press.

Munsch, R. (1981). *Jonathan Cleaned Up*. Toronto: Annick Press.

Munsch, R. (1982). *The Boy in the Drawer*. Toronto: Annick Press.

Munsch, R. (1982). *Mortimer*. Toronto: Annick Press.

Munsch, R. (1982). *Murmel Murmel Murmel*. Toronto: Annick Press.

Munsch, R. (1982). *Fire Station*. Toronto: Annick Press.

Munsch, R. (1983). *David's Father*. Toronto: Annick Press.

Munsch, R. (1984). *Millicent and the Wind*. Toronto: Annick Press.

Munsch, R. (1985). *Thomas' Snowsuit*. Toronto: Annick Press.

Munsch, R. (1986). *50 Below Zero*. Toronto: Annick Press.

Munsch, R. (1987). *I Have to Go!* Toronto: Annick Press.

Munsch, R. (1987). *Love You Forever*. Willowdale, Ontario: Firefly Books.

Munsch, R. (1987). *Moira's Birthday*. Toronto: Annick Press.

Munsch, R. (1988). *A Promise Is a Promise*. Toronto: Annick Press.

Munsch, R. (1988). *Angela's Airplane*. Toronto: Annick Press.

Munsch, R. (1989). *Pigs*. Toronto: Annick Press.

Munsch, R. (1990). *Good Families Don't*. Doubleday.

Munsch, R. (1990). *Something Good*. Toronto: Annick Press.

Munsch, R. (1991). *Matthew and the Midnight Tow Truck*. Toronto: Annick Press.

Munsch, R. (1991). *Show and Tell*. Toronto: Annick Press.

Munsch, R. (1991). *Agu, Agu, Agu: Murmel, Murmel, Murmel*. Toronto: Annick Press.

Munsch, R. (1992). *Jonathan Cleaned Up—Then He Heard a Sound, or Blackberry Subway Jam*. Toronto: Annick Press.

Munsch, R. (1992). *Purple Green and Yellow*. Toronto: Annick Press.

Munsch, R. (1992). *La Estaciòn de los Bonberos*. Toronto: Annick Press.

Munsch, R. (1992). *Siempre Te Querre*. Toronto: Annick Press.

Munsch, R. (1992). *Get Me Another One*. Toronto: Annick Press.

Munsch, R. (1993). *Wait and See*. Toronto: Annick Press.

Munsch, R. (1994). *Where Is Gah-ning?* Willowdale, Ontario: Firefly Books.

Munsch, R. (1995). *From Far Away*. Toronto: Annick Press.
Munsch, R. (1996). *Stephanie's Ponytail*. Toronto: Annick Press.
Munsch, R. (1996). *Andrew's Tooth*. Toronto: Annick Press.

Audio Tapes
Munsch: Favorite Stories. (1983).
Murmel Murmel Munsch (1985).
Love You Forever (1987).
More Munsch (1992).
Munsch: A Book on Tape—Vol. 1 (*Mortimer & The Paper Bag Princess*).
Munsch: A Book on Tape—Vol. 2 (*Angela's Airplane & Mudpuddle*).

Video Tapes
Robert Munsch (Canada Author's Series)
Robert Munsch Favorite Stories

Plays
Munsch, R. (1986). *The Paper Bag Princess and Other Stories*. Toronto: Annick Press.
Munsch, R. (1987). *Snowsuits, Birthdays and Giants*. Toronto: Annick Press.

*We shall not cease from exploration
and the end of all our exploring will be
to arrive where we started and know
the place for the first time.*

—T. S. Eliot

Appendices

Children enjoy writing letters to authors in response to reading their books, or to tell them personal stories, or to ask authors questions. All authors love to receive letters from children (and teachers!)

Many authors visit classrooms, provide workshops for students, or speak at Young Authors Conferences. The following list will assist you in contacting the authors in this book.

Artie Ann Bates
c/o Publicity Director
Houghton Mifflin Company
222 Berkely St.
Boston, MA 02116-3764

Lynne Cherry
c/o Harcourt Brace & Co.
15 E. 26th St.
New York, NY 10010

Sally Derby
c/o Walker & Company
435 Hudson St.
New York, NY 10014

Judy Finchler
c/o Walker & Company
435 Hudson St.
New York, NY 10014

Paul Brett Johnson
444 Fayette Park
Lexington, KY 40508
OR
c/o Orchard Books
95 Madison Ave.
New York, NY 10016

Marcia Thornton Jones
c/o Scholastic
555 Broadway
New York, NY 10012

Nancy Smiler Levinson
139 Coldwater Canyon Dr.
Beverly Hills, CA 90210
OR
c/o Scholastic
555 Broadway
New York, NY 10012

Celeste Lewis
c/o Orchard Books
95 Madison Ave.
New York, NY 10016

Paul Owen Lewis
P. O. Box 227
West Linn, OR 97068
(800) 538-3228
OR
c/o Beyond Words Publishing Inc.
20827 NW Cornell Road, Suite 500
Hillsboro, OR 97124-9808

George Ella Lyon
c/o Orchard Books
95 Madison Ave.
New York, NY 10016

Suse MacDonald
P. O. Box 25
South Londonderry, VT 05148
(802) 824-6107
e-mail: suse@create4kids.com
Have a web chat with Suse at her
website: http://www.create4kids.com

Contacting Authors

Betsy Maestro
74 Mile Creek Rd.
Old Lyme, CT 06371

Emily Arnold McCully
c/o Putnam & Grosset Group
200 Madison Ave.
New York, NY 10016

Megan McDonald
c/o Orchard Books
95 Madison Ave.
New York, NY 10016

Robert Munsch
c/o Writers' Union of Canada
24 Ryerson Ave.
Toronto, Ontario
Canada M5T 2P3

Naomi Shihab Nye
c/o Simon & Schuster
1230 Avenue of the Americas
New York, NY 10022

Jerrie Oughton
c/o Publicity Director
Houghton Mifflin Company
222 Berkely St.
Boston, MA 02116-3764

Joanne Rocklin
1830 Westholme Ave.
Los Angeles, CA 90025
OR
c/o Scholastic
555 Broadway
New York, NY 10012

Ann Whitford Paul
c/o Harcourt Brace & Co.
15 E. 26th St.
New York, NY 10010

Jill Wheeler
c/o Abdo & Daughters
6535 Cecelia Circle
Edina, MN 55439

Interesting resources on the Web for teachers about authors, books, and writing.

- http://author-illustr-source.com
  "Author-Illustrator Source"

  This website is a means by which educators can gather information about authors and illustrators, their books, and the types of school programs writers provide.

- http://www.acs.ucalgary.ca/~dkbrown
  "Children's Literature Web Guide"

  This website contains resources related to books for children, including "Resources for Teachers," "Authors on the Web," "Stories on the Web," and many more.

- http://www.amazon.com
  "Amazon Books"

  This site is a great resource for locating hard-to-find books and for searching for books by topic, author, illustrator, or title.

- http://www.carolhurst.com
  "Carol Hurst's Children's Literature Site"

  Website contains materials and activities that use literature to integrate themes across the curriculum.

Behn, R., & Twichell, C. (1992). *The Practice of Poetry*. New York: HarperCollins.

Bernays, A., & Painter, P. (1990). *What If?* New York: HarperCollins.

Bury, C. (1993). When all the right parts don't run the engine. *Language Arts*, *70*, 12–13.

Calkins, L. M. (1994). *The Art of Teaching Writing*. (New ed.). Portsmouth, NH: Heinemann Educational Books.

Cox, B. E., Shanahan, T., & Sulzby, E. (1990). Good and poor elementary readers' use of cohesion in writing. *Reading Research Quarterly*, *25*, 47–65.

Downing, S. (1995). Teaching writing for today's demands. *Language Arts*, *72*, 200–205.

Frank, M. (1979). *If You're Trying to Teach Kids How to Write, You've Gotta Have This Book!* Nashville, TN: Incentive Publications.

Goldberg, N. (1986). *Writing Down the Bones*. Boston, MA: Shambhala.

Graves, D. (1995). Sharing the tools of the writing trade: New ways to teach children conventions of punctuation. *Instructor*, *105*(4), 39–40.

Graves, D. (1983). *Writing: Teachers and Children at Work*. Exeter, NH: Heinemann Educational Books.

Hall, N. (1987). *The Emergence of Literacy*. Portsmouth, NH: Heinemann Educational Books.

Lamott, A. (1994). *Bird by Bird*. New York: Pantheon Books.

Macrorie, K. (1985). *Telling Writing* (4th ed.). Portsmouth, NH: Boynton/Cook Publishers.

Morrow, (1989). *Literacy Development in the Early Years: Helping Children Read and Write*. Englewood Cliffs, NJ: Prentice Hall.

Reutzel, D. R., & Cooter, R. B. (1990). Whole language: Comparative effects on first-grade reading achievement. *Journal of Educational Research*, *83*, 252–256.

Taylor, N. E., Blum, I. H., & Logsdon, M. (1986). The development of written language awareness: Environmental aspects and program characteristics. *Reading Research Quarterly*, *21*(2), 132–149.

References